BABY BONDING

GIVING YOUR CHILD A SECURE START TO LIFE

BABY BONDING

GIVING YOUR CHILD A SECURE START TO LIFE
Dr Jenny Sutcliffe

ORIGINAL PHOTOGRAPHY BY DON WOOD

Virgin

For Tara, Robert, Roshean, Owen & Matthew
and Nigel & Tom

———

First published in Great Britain 1994 by
Virgin Publishing Ltd.,
332, Ladbroke Grove,
London W10 5AH.

ISBN 1-85227-429-8

British Library Cataloguing in Publication Data is available from
the British Library

This book was conceived, edited, designed and produced by
Morgan Samuel Editions,
11 Uxbridge Street,
London W8 7TQ.

Typeset in Goudy at 10pt on 13pt.
Separated by Wace Corporate Imaging Ltd, London.
Printed and bound in Spain by Graficromo SA, Cordoba.

10 9 8 7 6 5 4 3 2

for Morgan Samuel Editions
Publisher: Nigel Perryman
Design: Tony Paine Design
Photography: Don Wood
Illustrator: Frances Lloyd
Managing Editor: Tim Probart
Editor: Lucy Berridge
Editorial: Loulou Brown; Christine Nelsen
Editorial assistants: Lorna Batty; Abigail Spurway; Michelle
Reedy
Picture research: Irene Lynch

This book is not intended to be a guide to the diagnosis, treatment or prognosis of any medical condition, whether physical or
psychological. In case of illness, consult your doctor.

Contents

Introduction

As soon as I had baby number three, friends started to tease, calling me a rabbit and an earth mother. But I also found that as friends became mothers for the first time, many would contact me asking for advice and help on caring for their child – not how to change a nappy, but "will I spoil him?", "why is he crying?" and "I'm going mad, no-one warned me" – assuming that a woman who had had five children from choice should know what she was talking about. Two years ago, one particular friend, Emma Worth, who works in publishing and was having her first child, started asking the normal questions – later she suggested I wrote this book.

My first thoughts were that the majority of things I had to say were all common-sense, and that as long as you loved your child you couldn't go far wrong. I still believe this, but the more I researched the subject of caring for the psychological development and health of children the more I realized that though there are many extremely good books and articles on the subject, the majority of those for the general public are based on the physical day-to-day care of a baby rather than its psychological development.

"Bonding" has become a fashionable word though one that is often misunderstood. Bonding is not instinctive, as many of us believe – think of the hideous and all too numerous reports of baby battering and abuse. Ideally, a baby and child would live with its two natural parents in love and harmony, but divorce, single parents and young inexperienced mothers are a reality, and as a divorced mother myself I have no right to moralise or pontificate – so all I've given are the facts, and possible ways of helping the situation. I've tried to write a practical book about an emotive subject and though I have researched widely, the thoughts are entirely my own.

Babies are individuals, some easier to care for and love than others. With one you might react intuitively in the correct way, your personalities naturally matching; with another you might clash and find things difficult. I hope that in this book you will find some suggestions that make these difficulties easier to understand and cope with, so that you can be sensitive to the needs of both yourself and your child. I have always liked children and I still do, but though I love all mine, I certainly haven't liked all of them all of the time and I am sure this is equally true of their feelings for me. You'll bond well with your children if, for the most part, you enjoy each other, take pleasure in each other's company and respect each other as individuals.

I'd like to thank Emma Worth not only for encouraging me to write this book but for all her support, the questions she has asked and the time she has taken with me. I would also like to thank Doctor Jane Bernal, a child psychiatrist, for her help with research material and her advice, though she is not responsible for any opinions expressed. Finally, this book would never have been completed without the assistance and bullying of Nigel Perryman, the humour and resilience of my children and a deadline.

Jenny Sutcliffe

I

Bonding In Theory

MUCH OF THIS BOOK is concerned with the
practical approach to bonding with your child,
and it suggests ways to help you and your family
make bonds that are secure and lasting – from
the start of pregnancy to the time
your child begins school.
But in this section I want to look at
the theory behind bonding. Forming
a firm bond with your child from an
early age is essential for his or her
future stability, but forging this bond
is not always as easy as many would
like to think and it's by no means
always an instinctive process. I hope that this
section will brush aside some of the
preconceptions that new parents may have.

What is Bonding?

"Bonding" has become something of a buzz word. But the trouble is that it means so many different things to different people: some seem to think that baby bonding is so natural that it's not worth worrying about, while child psychologists and sociologists have precise but often contradictory and confusing definitions. On the other hand, some dictionaries define bonding in terms of "restraint of freedom" and "slavery" – and many parents know only too well what is meant. In the next few pages I am going to try to define my terms and cut through some of the confusion.

For the purposes of this book, I am using a scientific definition of bonding that I hope is tinged with common sense. So – and perhaps what follows should be in italics, to make it look more important – *baby bonding is the process whereby as a result of on-going interaction between baby and parent (or baby and other family member) in which both play an active role, a mutual, loving, secure relationship is established that gives both parties emotional fulfilment, self-esteem, stability, a link of dependency (though, later, the ability to be independent) and the capacity to realize their potential in life.*

My apologies for the previous sentence. However, it is almost impossible to give a more concise definition of what is an extremely complex concept. And its very complexity – as well as the bulk of modern research – leads me to clench my teeth when I hear one common response to the mention of baby bonding: "Surely it's instinctive". It isn't. But I'm getting ahead of myself *(see pp.16-17)*. Remember, too, that bonding is a two-way street. Babies are born with inherent characteristics and personalities that will affect your response to your child as well as your child's reaction to you – they are not lumps of clay, waiting to be shaped by their parents.

Bonds and attachments

So what exactly is the nature of the bond that baby bonding produces? Yet again, the answer is complex – mainly because researchers, doctors and psychologists all use different terms to mean much the same thing; and magazine writers often compound the confusion by attaching unwarranted significance to these terms.

In general, doctors talk about the "bond" that parents have with a child, and use the word "attachment" to describe the bond a baby has with a parent. However, researchers in the fields of child psychology and behavioural studies use the word "attachment" to describe a parent's relationship with its child (as in the phrase "maternal attachment") and, generally, though not always, describe a child as forming a bond with its parents.

But these are all unnecessary distinctions. For the purposes of this book, I am going to use the word "bond" for preference, and alternate it with "attachment" only because it becomes rather boring to read the same word over and over again. But when the word "attachment" is qualified, it usually has a specific meaning – and you may well find such phrases in other books and magazines. Let me try to explain.

According to the theory, a baby can form one of three different types of attachment. The first is the true, secure bond: a baby that has a strong bond with you, for example, is secure enough to leave your side and play, either with other children or on its own – something that is vital for psychological development. But the second type of bond is called "anxiety attachment": lacking security, a child will constantly cling to its mother and follow her if she leaves the room. Such children often whine and moan, and are afraid of strangers; when they are ill, anxious, or feeling insecure, they display symptoms of anxiety attachment, though these

Left Secure bonding gives a child the confidence to play happily either alone or with friends, and to enjoy socializing with strangers.

Left Playground scuffles are are a normal part of childhood, but an overly aggressive child might be showing signs of inadequate bonding.

symptoms often disappear once the cause for anxiety has been removed. Of course, quite a few children become a little anxious when separated from their mothers – and this is quite normal – but when a child has no secure bond the degree of anxiousness exhibited is often abnormally high.

The third type of attachment, according to the researchers, is very curious indeed, because it doesn't exist: the child cannot form any type of bond with its mother, gives up trying to do so and becomes very independent. You might call this (and the phrase is my own, not from the research) "promiscuous attachment", because, again, the child becomes anxious but in this case seeks attention constantly: because there is no primary bond, the child has no basis on which to judge future attachments and often makes indiscriminate, short-term friendships that have little depth or basis.

Cultural conundrums

There's another complication: what I have just written – with deliberate references to mother and baby – would seem very strange to those brought up in non-industrialized, western cultures. To me, a two-parent, nuclear family in which the mother has the primary responsibility for child-raising is the norm; in fact, it seems the ideal. Therefore, I tend to assume that the primary, healthy and natural bond is between mother and child, or, in some cases, between father and child.

But family arrangements are completely different in many other parts of the world. One study showed that only three per cent of children in a survey covering 186 non-industrialized societies were cared for exclusively by their mothers. In such societies, it is not considered that a mother's ability to care for her child is necessarily any superior to that of other family members. Children brought up in these societies thrive, so we must conclude that our own cultural certainties are not as certain as all that. To us, life as an Ik baby in Northern Uganda seems appallingly disadvantaged (*see pp.22-3*), but large numbers of Ik babies still grow up and thrive.

Bondage of love

Having established my definition of a bond, there still remains the question of how bonding takes place. Of course, that is what this book is about; but at this point I'm going to give a quick summary of the essence of baby bonding.

The bonding process begins with your love for your baby. Babies who suffer from neglect, boredom or anxiety do not feel sufficiently secure to form a bond with their parents. But bonding involves more than just feeding and bathing: if you only respond to your baby's most obvious needs, bonding won't take place. Bonding occurs when you learn to be sensitive even to very subtle cues, such as facial expressions and arm movement: in fact, many parents gain the ability to predict their children's actions just by watching their behaviour carefully. The best way to form a bond with your baby is to pay close attention to what he or she is trying to say through body language, as well as responding to more obvious cues, such as crying or gurgling.

Multiple bonds

Many psychologists have argued over whether a baby can bond with more than one person. Eminent English psychologist Dr John Bowlby (1907-1990) said in a paper published by the World Health Organization in 1951 that while babies may respond to affection shown by others, they are unable to form a close, strong bond with more than one person. Bowlby also stated that children who cannot form a strong bond with their mothers are more likely to suffer psychological problems later in their lives.

But recent studies dispute Bowlby's findings. Today, most child specialists believe that once a child's primary bond has formed, further bonds will develop easily. By the time your baby is between one and two years old, multiple bonds will have developed. The first bond is very important, as it becomes the basis for all the child's future bonds, but whether it takes place with the mother, father, or even someone else doesn't matter.

There are several reasons why it is important for a child to have multiple bonds – ideally four or five. First, if it turns out that the primary attachment figure cannot be with the child – if, for example, a child's mother goes to hospital to have another baby – the child may become very distressed if the mother is the only person with whom a bond has been formed. Second, because multiple bonds give a child variety in relationships and extra stimulation.

Cue a tantrum

For our purposes, the process of bonding can best be defined as a continuous interaction between baby and parent in which both play an active role. The roles change over the first year of a baby's life. For the first six months, your baby's innate survival instincts guide the relationship. Because babies cannot survive on their own, they are born with the ability to tell adults how they are feeling. At first, your baby can only communicate by crying, but later on smiling, gurgling, and tantrum-throwing are added to its range of techniques.

Babies are unable to form attachments until they are about six months old, because it's only by then that the pathways of the brain have developed sufficiently, so bonding will be a one-way street at the beginning. Your baby will be most comfortable with a familiar carer, but will respond to anyone who attends to his or her needs: there is absolutely no evidence that child-care regimes – however fashionable they may be – have any effect whatsoever on bonding or later psychological development. For our purposes, it really doesn't matter whether you breastfeed or not, or when you start to potty-train; what is important is your attitude. Once you have proved your love, consistency, stability and capacity to react to cues a mutual bond will form. Most children have formed a bond with what researchers call a "primary attachment figure" by the time they are about eight months old – about 50 per cent with their mothers, 33 per cent with their fathers and 17 per cent with other individuals.

Above Multiple bonding is important to prevent a child from becoming solely dependent on the focus of primary attachment. Playing with other members of the family is an ideal way for a child to form such bonds and learn to interact with other people.

Bonding in the Family

As well as using the words "bond" and "attachment" in varying ways, psychologists draw distinctions between the different types of attachment that form between family members and a child, from the side of the family. The three main types cover the relationships between mother and child, father and child, and siblings and child – the differences between them being based on biology and practicality rather than preconceptions about gender roles.

Maternal attachment

Curiously, very little research is available to tell us about the mother's side of the mother-child bond. A few facts are certain, though: first, women are genetically programmed and biologically equipped to be attracted to infants, and, in most cases, their environment from childhood onwards strengthens and increases this tendency. Second, the vast majority of women (though by no means all, *see pp.16-17*) have an instinctive love for their children – to varying degrees, however, because some mothers fall madly and helplessly in love with their babies the moment they first look into their eyes, while others find that love only develops its full passion and intensity over a number of months or years. Third, for most women this love can be defined as a fiercely protective emotional attachment that heightens normal emotions, such as anxiety for a baby's well-being, possessiveness and so on, and grows in strength as the bond becomes increasingly firmly established over time.

To a certain extent, a mother's emotions are triggered by the release of the "mothering hormones", prolactin and oxytocin, which are produced at birth (*see pp.42-43*). But much of a mother's relationship with her child seems to depend on an interaction between biological instinct and early environment: mothers whose childhood has been emotionally deprived find that the instinct is less strong.

Fathers

Strong – even passionate – feelings of attachment are not just the prerogative of mothers: most fathers have a sense of oneness with their children, too. Often, there is a patriarchal element in this – a feeling that the father's line and genes are being perpetuated. But proper bonding takes time, and even though fathers lack the purely biochemical reflexes that help them develop the process, a father who is

Below The mother-child bond may form at birth, or take a little longer. The majority of women, though, have instinct – as well as hormones – to help them to love and protect their new-born babies.

encouraged to help with his baby's care from the beginning can form an attachment that is just as strong as that of the mother.

At first some new fathers feel uncomfortable around their babies and shy away from holding them, worrying that they will make mistakes. But the more time a father spends with the baby, the stronger his attachment will become. A man cannot breast feed a baby, but he can still play a part in changing, bathing, and cuddling the baby. Fathers who have frequent contact with their babies become more comfortable with them, and learn how to read their cues. And fathers who work all day often spend more time in stimulating one-to-one interactions in the evening than mothers who stay at home, because they have fewer distractions.

Brothers and sisters

Much research has been conducted on the effect of a lack of a mother-child bond, and a little on the lack of a paternal bond, but what

Above The paternal bond often takes longer to develop than the mother-child bond, but once formed it is usually equally strong.

about sibling attachment? A number of studies have been carried out into the effect of separation of a child from both parents, but these tend not to consider the additional effect of separation from brothers and sisters in cases where there are more than one child. But one (Heinicke & Westheimer, 1965) showed that young children who were placed in institutionalized care suffered less problems and trauma if brothers and sisters were also admitted. Other studies have shown that an upset child's response to a sibling is similar to the response to a parent: the presence of any familiar person helps calm the child. So experts now believe that the child-sibling bond is of the same nature as the child-parent bond, though not always as important during childhood.

No bond is purely instinctive *(see pp.16-17)*, and this applies in particular to siblings. Brothers and sisters usually feel jealous of a new child *(see pp.82-83)*, and sometimes this jealousy turns into active dislike, but conflicts tend to lessen in frequency as the children grow older. But if siblings do form bonds, they are nearly always very strong ones. That is because a child doesn't feel the same type of responsibility towards a brother or sister that a parent does to a son or daughter. So the attachment that grows between siblings develops by choice, and usually lasts well into adulthood. You should encourage your children to bond, but you won't be able to force them.

Right Sibling bonds don't always develop, but when they do they tend to be very strong ones – to the benefit of both baby and child.

Is Bonding Instinctive?

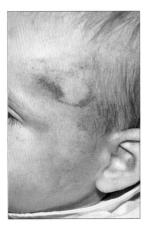

Below All-too-frequent incidences of baby battering tend to give the lie to the idea that baby bonding is instinctive.

One of the difficulties in writing a book about bonding is that I have to talk simultaneously about bonding from the point of view of both the baby and the parents, with the position of brothers and sisters as an added complication. And nowhere does this become more difficult than in the consideration of instinct.

I said earlier that people often say "Isn't it instinctive?" when they hear the phrase "Baby Bonding". They are generally referring to the bond between parent and child. But the process isn't instinctive: if it was, how can we explain battered babies and the horrifying rates of child abuse today? How do we account for the practice of infanticide over the ages – a habitual solution to the inconvenience of large families in Ancient Rome, and, according to some reports, prevalent in the case of new-born girls in rural China and India to this day?

The answer is that mothers and fathers have instincts that help promote bonding *(see pp.14-15)*, but a true bond is formed by adults as a result of cuddling, touching, stimulation and the communication that occurs when parents respond appropriately to the instinctive urges they feel, all over a long period. Instinct might promote proper bonding, but its force can be reduced by the environmental component of a parent's own upbringing, as well as by the environment into which a new child is born. For an extreme example, look at the Ik tribe, in Uganda *(see pp.22-23)*; in our own western culture, though, look at the proven tendency for adults who have been abused during their own childhood to abuse their own children; and also the desperate effects that poverty, single parenthood and material deprivation can have on emotional well-being.

Right Constant crying can put a strain on any mother's instinct towards bonding with her baby, especially when there have been difficulties in her own childhood. But it's vitally important to persevere, and provide the baby with the stimulation that is so necessary for bonding.

Of course, all of this is a matter of degree. Generally, responsive, mature adults who enjoy stability in their relationship and reasonably comfortable economic circumstances bond quite naturally and easily. What is at question – and it's the secondary question – in this book is the degree to which they bond.

An instinct for survival

My primary concern in *Baby Bonding* is to show how babies can be helped to form proper bonds that benefit them throughout life *(see pp.18-21)*. A major part of the process of forming a bond is dependent on the behaviour of parents. But babies have their own input, too, and instinct is what rules them.

Many parents will feel extremely uncomfortable with the thoughts that follow. Inconveniently, though – and I must admit that it makes me feel uneasy – the fact is that babies are not born with an instinctive emotional attachment to their parents. Of course, in biological terms this is sensible: a baby's first instinct must be for survival, and that means doing everything that it can – screaming, crying, cooing, gurgling, throwing tantrums and so on – to endear itself to whoever might be available to care for it. As far as a baby is concerned, "out of sight" means "out of mind", because a baby's brain is not sufficiently mature to form an emotional attachment or bond until around the age of six months.

When babies do start to form bonds, these are not necessarily with the person primarily concerned with their day-to-day care – which might be efficient but lacking in warmth and sensitivity – but with the person who stimulates them the most and responds most appropriately to their changing moods. That is why parents who have nannies or use creches, and so don't see their children all day, can still provide the primary bond. It is also why, as I said earlier, some 17 per cent of eight-month-old babies have a primary bond with someone other than their mother or father: in these cases it is likely that someone other than the parents has given them the most sensitive stimulation and proved the most trustworthy in reacting to their cues quickly and efficiently.

Of course, once the baby has matured sufficiently for a primary bond to be formed, the normal instincts of humanity for love, recognition and special relationships gain expression. So relationships develop, especially with those who are most evident in their lives, such as parents and siblings – but only if the groundwork has been laid.

Below A baby will form its primary bond with the person that provides the most stimulation and responds best to its needs and moods. And with this bond in place, love, recognition and special relationships can grow.

Why Bonding is Important

There's a general agreement among researchers – in itself a rare thing – that the quality of an infant's first relationships is strongly associated with healthy psychological growth and that a strong bond with at least one carer provides a baby with the stability needed for healthy development. This consensus has been reached following an impressive amount of research. To give some examples (details are given at the end of the book, if you want to follow these up):

- an American study in 1983 (Sroufe) showed that babies who had not bonded well with a carer by the time they were a year old showed significantly more signs of antisocial behaviour and were more attention-seeking at the age of four-and-a-half than children who had formed secure bonds;

- research in 1988 (Howes, Rodning, Balluzzo & Myers) revealed that children with insecure bonds with their primary carer spent less time interacting with their peers than those with secure bonds. The same study demonstrated that insecurely bonded children engaged in less sophisticated play than securely bonded children. This indicates that a secure bond might also help your child's intellectual development;

- a 1985 study (Lütkenhaus, Grossman & Grossman) concluded that securely bonded children were more likely to stick with a difficult task, whereas insecurely bonded children became frustrated quickly and were easy to distract.

Below A strong bond gives a toddler the confidence to explore and play – and the resilience to try again even if something goes wrong the first time, as long as there's a comforting arm to lean on between times.

These are specific findings, but there are also a number of general conclusions that can be summed up in one sentence: the nature of a baby's primary bond forms the basis for all further relationships during life.

Bonding for the future

But why should this be so? There are a number of answers. First, a secure bond grows from and encompasses your baby's belief that he or she can trust you and depend on you. So a securely bonded baby becomes accustomed to finding relationships a source of comfort, reassurance and love. But an insecurely bonded baby becomes anxious, because he or she learns that people can't always be trusted, and becomes wary of entering into relationships. Second, children who are able to form strong bonds with their parents feel secure and protected, spend less time feeling anxious, and are more independent. As a result, they spend more time exploring on their own and playing, and are more receptive to new information and ideas.

Left A well-bonded child has the ability to concetrate on a difficult task and to persist until his attempts meet with success. Curiously, boys tend to be less persistent than girls – possibly because they are more easily affected by the stress of frustration.

Below A child who is bonding well does not seek constant attention, but is happy to play quietly alone, exploring and discovering, when you need to get on with something else.

To be fair, the research does not imply that all children who have secure bonds with their parents will grow into social, active, intelligent, well-adjusted adults, or that all those with insecure bonds will become antisocial and have psychological problems. Factors such as individual temperament and family environment also play a large part in determining a child's personality and development. The sex of a child makes a difference, too – many studies have shown that boys are more susceptible to stress than girls. But the research does demonstrate fairly convincingly that at the very least securely bonded children have a head start in healthy psychological growth.

Short-term gains

In addition to its long-term benefits, bonding brings immediate gains for both parents and baby. Mothers, fathers and their babies begin bonding when the parents start to respond to their babies' cues (*see Box overleaf*). As the cue-response pattern develops, parents become confident that they can respond to their child's needs effectively, and the child becomes confident that he or she can make the correct signals. Both parents and baby become more relaxed with each other and less anxious, which in turn allows trust and closeness to grow.

If you have a close bond with your baby, parenting will certainly become less difficult. It becomes easier to provide the constant care a baby requires when you feel you are doing a good job. Nothing and nobody can teach you how to be a good parent – and certainly not overnight – but forming a secure bond early in your relationship with your baby can help speed up the learning process.

Opposite Brothers and sisters may grow up to tease each other, and even fight, but they can also offer each other support and advice and present a united front to the world outside the family – and sometimes to parents as well.

Call me sister

Researchers have found that babies become capable of making multiple bonds between their first and second years (*see Multiple bonds, p.12*). Although the parent-child bond is the first relationship a child makes, bonds with other family members can be extremely beneficial. Sibling rivalry is rarely a problem if brothers and sisters are able to form close bonds with one another, and a child who has a close, loving relationship with a brother or sister is assured of a constant playmate and confidant. Siblings will inevitably tease each other, but although the taunts may sometimes seem to border on cruelty, a child that has bonded securely learns not to take a sibling's teasing too seriously: such children know that while there may be lots teasing or rivalry within the family, brothers and sisters will support them in the outside world.

Your children's relationships with one another may also help your relationship with them, because the time you spend with your children will be more enjoyable if they all get along and respect each other – even if it doesn't always seem that way from the outside. Two of my children are of the same sex and close in age – they fight continuously and noisily. But woe betide anyone – including me – who criticizes one of them, because the other will leap to their defence. They also talk very proudly about their brothers and sisters – but not in their presence.

If a child is upset about something you've done or said, a sibling can offer support and advice. While you may not enjoy the prospect of your children ganging up on you, it's added security for them. Acting together enables them to keep the lines of communication open. It's easier for a child to speak up if there's a loving brother or sister playing a supporting role – or a sibling may speak up for the child. This loyalty to each other becomes increasingly important during adolescence, when even the closest parents and children may have trouble understanding each other.

Responding to cues

Throughout this book, I talk about the importance of recognizing a child's cues and acting upon them, and show how this is vital to so many aspects of bonding. The cue-response element of bonding also helps a child develop, because babies learn patterns of behaviour through experience and mimicry.

If you hold a toy above your baby, for example, the baby will instinctively wave both arms and legs in order to try to touch it. Eventually – and perhaps with a bit of help from the mother – the baby's hand will hit the toy. The next time the baby tries to touch a toy, the hand movement will be stronger, and the baby will wave its hands more than its legs. Each time your baby is successful, the pattern will be reinforced, until the movement is learned.

Babies learn other behaviour patterns this way, too. A hungry baby will cry, often furiously, to tell you that he or she wants to be fed. If you respond to the cry quickly, the baby learns that crying will bring food in response, and as this action-reaction is learnt the child will not feel the need to cry so loudly. But a baby who is left to "cry it out" will not understand that communication with you is possible and will feel helpless and anxious – the crying is then not only for food but also the result of frustration, anger and anxiety. If allowed to get into a frenzy, the baby won't remember what the reason for crying was in the first place, and the knowledge that crying can be used to signal something very specific will be lost. A baby whose cries are responded to quickly by an adult learns that he or she has some control.

Babies also learn to associate facial expressions with appropriate emotions from the way you react to their smiles or grimaces. If you respond quickly to all these cues you will teach your baby to associate you with the easing of hunger or loneliness, and trust will develop.

Bonding in Other Cultures

I n western society, we tend to take many characteristics of the bonding process for granted – wrongly, as I hope I have shown. But in many other, non-western, cultures bonding is indeed a natural process: mainly in communities that remain close-knit with the extended family intact.

In such cultures, parenting is not as exclusive as it is in western societies. We tend to think of our children almost as possessions, and consider leaving them in the care of others an unfortunate necessity at best. But in small villages or poor inner-city areas, families live very near one another, or even share living units. Children are seen as the responsibility of all adults, and often "share" mothers. Child abuse is extremely rare in such situations, because there are many people involved in the daily care of a child, and one of them can take over and provide the primary bond if the child's mother cannot; multiple bonds are readily available, too. In Jamaica, for example, few children live in orphanages because an aunt, grandmother, sister or even a neighbour is nearly always available if the mother dies or proves to be an unfit parent.

Working patterns in such communities also tend to promote bonding. Indian and African mothers, who work in the fields, spend all day with their babies carried in saris, or swathed in cloth and straddled on a hip. This means that the baby is in constant contact with the mother, sharing her daily experience and interacting with others.

Below *In this Sudanese "shared" family, brothers, sisters, mothers, and wives all live under the roof of the male head of the family, and share responsibility for all the children.*

The other side of the coin

In some cultures, though, the concept of baby bonding would be thought a complete irrelevancy, if, indeed, it was known at all. Generally, these cultures are poor, primitive and unsuccessful. An extreme example comes from a small tribe in Northern Uganda, called the Ik. Leading a harsh, impoverished life, the Ik are barely capable of sustaining themselves. Under these conditions, the parent-child bond we consider natural does not develop. Children are turned out of the house to fend for themselves at the age of three, and the death of a child is a relief to the Ik: there is one less person competing for scarce resources.

A slightly less rigorous approach is shown in isolated Indian villages in Guatemala, where mothers keep their babies with them at all times, but rarely talk to them or play. There is very little interaction between mother and child during the first year or so of life – the belief is that babies are weak and will get sick easily, so they are kept indoors and not allowed to crawl. By the time they are one, these children are usually fearful, quiet and inactive. There are no long-term physical effects, but insufficient work has been done to assess the emotional effects of this treatment.

Above This Javanese mother, like women in many non-industrial societies, carries her baby in a sling as a matter of course. The constant contact between the two is an ideal way of promoting bonding.

However, there is some historical evidence that a lack of attention to bonding within a culture can be detrimental. An experiment was conducted in Oneida, America, in the mid-1800s: members of the Oneida Community believed in community living and what was then called "free love" – a 19th-century euphemism for open sexual promiscuity. Members of the community were expected to belong to each other equally, and partnerships such as marriage were frowned on because they were considered too exclusive. Children also belonged to the community, and a baby's parents were only allowed to live together for a short time before and after the birth. A baby was cared for full-time by its mother for the first nine months, and at night only for the next nine months. At 18 months children were sent to live with the other children of the community, with whom they were forbidden to form attachments, and any mother whose child seemed attached to her was publicly and formally criticized. Not unexpectedly, one visitor to the community reported that although the children were well cared for, they also seemed to be "subdued and desolate".

Even in more modern, industrialized cultures, conceptions of bonding often differ from our own. In Stalinist Russia, for example, the value of birth bonding was completely disregarded. Babies were taken from their mothers immediately after birth and kept in nurseries because it was believed that a mother would be likely to infect her baby if allowed to handle it too much. Babies were always fed by the clock, so the first, most natural cue-response pattern between mother and baby was eliminated – the idea was that a baby fed on demand would grow up to be undisciplined, and, therefore, a source of potential danger to the state.

Preconceptions

During pregnancy, you'll probably read books on parenting, buy baby clothes, think about names and decorate a nursery – all the while daydreaming about what your child will be like and what kind of parent you will be. You'll also probably attend classes and prepare a birth plan in anticipation of the big event. But in spite of all this planning and thought, most new parents aren't prepared for the reality of childbirth and are overwhelmed by all the new responsibilities of parenthood.

One reason is the decline of the extended family in our modern industrial society (*see pp.76-77*). As a result of this, some new mothers have never even touched a new-born baby, let alone been responsible for changing and bathing one. Without practical experience of the reality of childbirth and child-rearing, many parents have to rely on preconceptions, which often leave them psychologically unprepared for what is to come.

Dream babies

These preconceptions often start with the birth process. Mothers who are encouraged to work out a birth plan are often disappointed if things don't work out as expected – an emergency Caesarean or forceps delivery can cause emotional as well as physical damage (*see pp.54-55*). And even the sight of a baby whose birth has been comparatively easy may

Below It's rare indeed to find a picture-book baby like this – one that either sleeps peacefully or gurgles sweetly when awake. But this is the idealistic image that many parents-to-be carry in their minds.

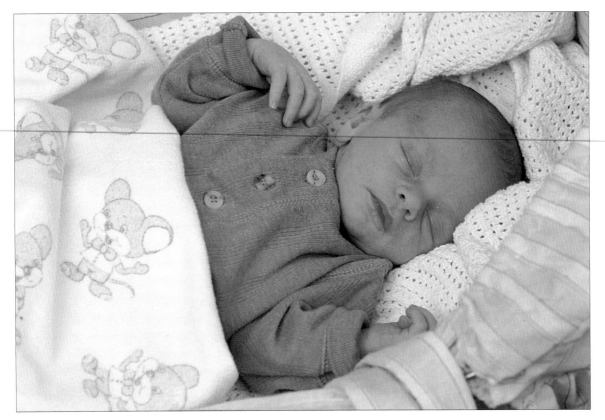

be unsettling to the parents: new-borns often have wrinkled skin, which is covered with blood and a creamy white substance, called vernix. Their skull bones aren't yet fused, so their heads are often an unusual shape as a result of being squeezed through the birth canal. Often, babies are slightly jaundiced, with yellow skin. In these circumstances, it's understandable if the parents' first response is far from the excitement, joy, love and immediate closeness that was expected, and this lack can cause feelings of guilt.

Although some mothers do connect instantly with their child, many take a little longer to begin to form a bond. Sometimes a mother is too exhausted or drugged to be able to cope with holding her child right away. Try not to be too worried if this should happen – you'll have plenty of time to get to know your new-born baby later.

Once home, other expectations come into play. Often they are based on media images of plump, cherubic, happy, clean children. Many new mothers and fathers also have preconceptions about perfect parents: mothers are content, calm, smiling women, gazing adoringly at their babies; fathers are supportive and helpful, but don't intrude into the precious mother-child bond, which exists from birth.

Of course, our preconceptions don't include a scene that is a little closer to reality: a tired, moody mother, changing the sixth messy nappy of the day with housework piling up around her. It's no wonder that new mothers feel overwhelmed when they find that their lives have been turned upside down, and that the peaceful, happy moments they've expected seem few and far between. Their former colleagues and friends are probably uninterested in their problems. Often new mothers are taken by surprise by the emotional ups and downs they experience in the first few weeks after birth. One moment they feel resentful of the new demands and lack of freedom; the next they feel guilty; and then they are suddenly overcome with love as the baby coos or smiles.

Above When reality strikes: the feeling of drowning in dirty nappies and unwashed dishes can be overwhelming as a new mother's emotions are turned upside down in the first few weeks after the birth of a new baby.

A last resort

Some couples decide to have a child because they think babies are cure-alls for failing relationships. In fact, babies can even put a strain on healthy relationships. Fathers sometimes feel they come a distant second to the new baby *(see pp.78-79)* – and reasonably so, because if both baby and partner want a mother's attention, the baby is going to win out. Some mothers become completely caught up with their new babies, and can't be bothered with looking attractive or with sex – especially if they're not getting enough support from their partner; fathers often feel an increased sense of responsibility and pressures to be better breadwinners. All these factors, in addition to tiredness and anxiety, can combine to alienate partners when they should be pulling together.

II

BONDING DURING PREGNANCY

PREGNANCY IS A TIME of mental adjustment for both parents, and for some mothers-to-be it can also be a time of doubt and discomfort. To alleviate worries, prepare yourself for the birth of your child in as many ways as possible: learn about the miracle that takes place in a mother's womb; keep your mind and body relaxed with music and exercise; and think about ways of making your home a warm and welcoming place for your new baby.
Such preparations will not only help make pregnancy a time of joyful expectation, but will also be the first vital steps in the bonding process.
Research shows that babies respond to signals from outside the womb from an early age, and the knowledge that your unborn baby is aware of your mood and the music you are listening to can help make pregnancy a highly rewarding experience.

A Parasite or a Joy?

Below A routine scan
provides a valuable
opportunity to forge a link
between the mother and the
unborn baby she is carrying;
the recognizably human
features a scan reveals help
dispel the idea of the baby as
a parasite.

Pregnancy can be a time of emotional highs and lows, and during the low times one of the most common feelings experienced by mothers-to-be (to whom these two pages are addressed) is that the baby is a parasite growing inside them and draining all their mental and physical resources.

An unborn baby is a parasite, it's true – nestling in the protective comfort of the womb it feeds off its mother, and, seemingly, gives nothing in return. However, not every type of parasite is an alien creature that harms its host. An unborn baby's relationship with its mother is not parasitic, but symbiotic – which means that it existence is beneficial to its host: it gives as well as takes, just like the bacteria in your intestine, which feed off you but aid digestion. But what does your unborn baby give you in return? Nothing concrete, it's true – though the embryo stimulates production of two hormones, progesterone and oestrogen, that soften and relax smooth muscles (which control involuntary movements), making the body ready for pregnancy and childbirth, and, later, the production of prostaglandins, which prepare the birth canal for labour.

What your unborn baby can give you is dependent on your receptivity. It is up to you to put yourself in touch with the essential humanity of your baby: to think of it as a human being in the process of creation; an embryonic person that is part of both you and of your partner but which will have its own separate identity.

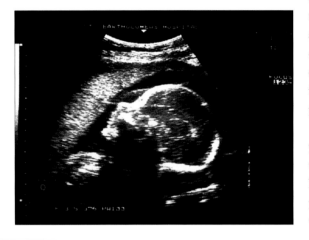

Right Modern technology
gives both parents the
opportunity to see their
child developing in the
womb and allows the baby
to become a part of their
lives long before the birth.

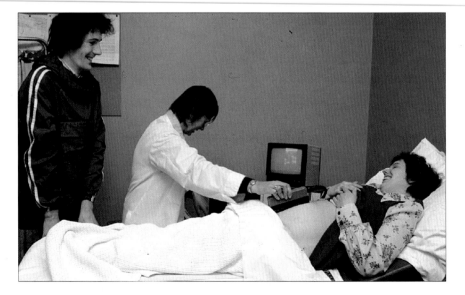

Considered coldly – and especially when you're being sick – such sentiments seem a little overblown. Pregnancy is a question of attitudes, though. If you take the trouble to think about how your baby is growing inside you, and contemplate the future you will have together, it becomes much easier to believe that your baby is giving you something in return and to get rid of the idea that it is a parasite.

Life in the womb

In order to appreciate the humanity of your unborn baby, it's helpful to know how quickly a single cell grows into what is recognizable as a human being, so you can visualize what is going on inside you.

A baby develops rapidly in the womb: it starts to make spontaneous movements at around eight weeks from conception (though you won't be able to feel them until the fourth month). If you could see inside yourself, you would see your baby sucking its thumb and fingers from about the tenth week and swallowing and peeing from around eleven weeks; you would notice your baby reacting to the sound of your voice between the twelfth and twentieth week *(see pp.30-31)* and watch facial expressions, such as looking, smiling and grimacing, from around eight months.

If it were possible, you would see your baby react to your changing emotions, too. You release a hormone called adrenaline (known as epinephrine in America), whenever you are under physical or mental stress – it's often called the "flight or fight" hormone. Adrenaline can pass across the placenta to the baby and increases its level of activity – by as much as ten times more than normal if the stress is prolonged.

But the brain produces another set of hormones, called endorphins, that counter stress and act as the body's own pain-killers and tranquillizers. Endorphins affect your emotions and promote feelings of calmness and happiness; they pass across the placenta, too, causing the same effect in your baby and are produced throughout pregnancy in ever-increasing amounts, peaking at child birth. Relaxation and contentment increase the amount of endorphins in the system, and so help you to enjoy your pregnancy.

You'll find out how to avoid stress during pregnancy, and so reduce adrenaline levels, and promote relaxation, to increase endorphin levels, later on in this book *(see pp.32-37)*. Follow this advice, and try to visualize the wonder of what is happening inside you: it can make a big difference to whether you think of your unborn baby as a parasite or a joy.

Above A baby starts to hear, move and react to changes in its environment much earlier in pregnancy than was once thought. To feel the baby moving, while visualizing its life within the womb, can help make pregnancy a time of fulfilment for both mother

Music

As technology advances, scientists are discovering more and more about what life in the womb is like. Many medical specialists used to believe that a baby's senses did not develop until after birth, but most now agree that sensory awareness starts to develop in the womb, and does so much faster than had previously been imagined. And this increases the importance of any sensory input that can be provided during pregnancy.

Hearing before birth

Some of the most recent – and the most fascinating – studies that have been carried out on unborn babies involve the ability to hear and to recognize sounds that are repeated often. It is now known that a foetus starts to be able to hear sometime between 12 and 20 weeks from conception. Unborn babies can hear the mother's heartbeat, her voice, sounds from her digestive tract, her breathing, and the rushing of her blood. The baby can also hear sounds from the other side of the abdominal wall, such as the father's voice, and

Right *Music can be wonderfully soothing for both an expectant mother and her unborn baby, and provides a means of communication, so that bonding can start even before birth.*

music. Studies show that babies recognize these sounds after birth: for example, one investigation showed that new-borns preferred – which means that they became more excited and their heartbeats quickened – listening to stories their mothers had read to them while still in the womb to stories they had not heard before.

Soothing in the womb

This ability to hear in the womb and to remember what was heard later is obviously important when it comes to music – especially when you consider the power music has to alter moods. Researchers have shown that soothing melodies with a steady rhythm, such as classical music or blues, help soothe most babies, while many kick and become restless if rock music is played. One study, at Queen's University, in Belfast, Northern Ireland, showed that 36-week-old foetuses who had been played a tune twice a day since the time they had been conceived reacted as if they recognized it – usually by becoming more active inside the womb; they reacted differently if played an unfamiliar tune. After birth, the babies seemed to recognize the tune, and some mothers found that they could be soothed by familiar music.

This means that mothers can communicate with their unborn babies, so the all-important process of bonding can start even before birth. And music is one of the most enjoyable ways in which you can share your daily life with your baby: music that calms and soothes the mother will also calm and soothe the foetus. This is not just an aural effect, though. An expectant mother who is under stress produces increased levels of certain hormones, which can be detected by the foetus. The unborn baby can also sense the mother's emotions because of changes in her voice and heartbeat, and will react to the mother's stress by becoming stressed itself. So a baby is liable to be very active and kick a lot in the womb if the mother is tense, anxious and excitable. But if the mother is calm and relaxed, so will the baby be. And the more relaxed both are, the easier it will be for a bond to form.

Below Remarkably, when you read to your toddler during your pregnancy, your unborn baby can hear the sound and rhythm of your voice. After birth, babies often seem to recognize stories heard in the womb.

Only communicate

Some mothers might well feel rather silly when talking to their stomachs, even though, as I've said, babies appear to react familiarly to stories told while they are still in the womb. If you feel uncomfortable with the idea, try singing. My children all leave the room if I sing, but for many women, singing and humming through the day is completely natural. Otherwise play recorded music of a type that makes you feel happy and relaxed.

Remember, too that the baby can also hear its father's voice – in fact, it is believed that the lower-pitched tones of a male voice can be heard more clearly by the foetus than a high-pitched female voice. The realization that your baby is listening to you and will remember the sound you make can be a turning point in pregnancy. And thinking of your baby as a real person who can hear you can only strengthen your future bond, and help give the child a basis of secure familiarity with you after it is born.

Learning to Relax

At the beginning of this section I looked at how any stress that you, as an expectant mother, experience may affect your unborn baby *(see pp.28-29)*. It's difficult, but your aim must be to maintain a mental and physical equilibrium, in order to reduce the levels of adrenaline (epinephrine in America), which is produced by worry and fear on your part and increases the baby's activity, and increase the levels of endorphins, which are produced when you are relaxed and content to soothe and relax your baby.

It's easy to say this, of course, but how do you achieve it? A positive attitude is a good start – and I hope that what you have been reading in this book will go some way to help you reduce anxiety and acquire this. But the best way to approach the problem is to set time aside for relaxation, using any or all of the techniques discussed on the following pages: muscular relaxation; posture, yoga, massage and swimming. These basic relaxation techniques release the tension in your muscles and help ensure deep, regular breathing and correct posture, so lowering adrenaline levels and increasing endorphins.

Please make sure that you do make time for relaxation, though. It's all too easy to let things slip, especially when you're busy and tired, and it is vital that both you and your baby relax if you are to enjoy your pregnancy.

Muscular relaxation

Below Before starting on muscular relaxation, put on comfortable clothes, choose a warm, quiet room and lie down, either on the floor or a firm bed; support your knees with a cushion if it feels more comfortable. Then take up the basic relaxation position.

The aim of this technique is to relax all your muscles one by one, while letting your mind go blank, and breathing deeply and regularly. But before you do this, you should take up the basic relaxation position, shown in the photograph below.

First of all, tense the muscles of your toes on both feet; hold the tense position for a few seconds and then let the toes flop. Repeat this several times. Then tense both legs tightly; hold and let go – if someone lifted up your legs at this point and released them they should fall down without any resistance on your part. Using the same technique on each set of muscles, work up the body to your head – from toes to thighs, to buttocks, and so on – and feel the muscles become pleasantly warm and heavy. Don't move to a new set of muscles until the ones you are working on feel completely relaxed.

Continue up the body – don't forget to include the stomach – then move to the arms and up through the shoulders and neck to the head. There is often a lot of built-up tension in the shoulder and neck muscles, so hunch the shoulders up towards the ears, pull the shoulder blades together and rotate your shoulders – first clockwise, then anti-clockwise – and hold and let go after each movement. Relaxing your face poses more of a problem, but try tensing the muscles by grimacing and then letting them go.

Posture

It's remarkable how few people sit, stand or walk with correct posture. In most cases, bad habits tend to set in during childhood, and soon become so entrenched that they feel completely normal. And these habits are often emphasized during pregnancy, as a mother's body changes shape to accommodate her growing baby.

Throughout our evolution, the spine has adapted to our upright posture by curving in a slight "S" shape. If the curve is allowed to become more pronounced through bad posture, pressure on the lower spine increases, causing low-back pain and tension. It also means that the full weight of the baby is carried by the stomach muscles and ligaments, and not, as it should be, by the pelvis and the pelvic muscles. On the other hand, if the curve becomes too flattened, the baby will be carried too far back in the body, and this can also result in low-back pain.

During pregnancy the curvature of the spine increases gently anyway, into order to compensate for the weight of the baby in front, which makes it even more important to adopt a correct posture if problems are to be avoided. Practise standing or kneeling in the positions shown on this page. If you have a problem consult a teacher of the Alexander Technique (a method of achieving and maintaining correct posture) – but make sure you choose one who is properly qualified.

Left Good posture is vital to relaxation in pregnancy. When the curve of the spinal column is correct, weight is distributed evenly and there is no strain; the upper spine is free of tension, which helps breathing and makes you feel you're walking tall.

Below Kneeling on all fours can ease tension in the back. Try rocking back on to your heels from this position to increase flexibility, or go forwards towards the floor. Make sure your back is straight, raise your head slowly to ease neck tension, arch your back like a cat and then lower your back so that your bottom sticks out.

Yoga

The word "yoga" means "union", and when practising this technique the aim is to achieve a balance between the physical, mental and spiritual attributes of an individual. This is beneficial at all times of life, but during pregnancy there are additional benefits, because yoga techniques combine relaxation with breathing control and tone the body muscles, so preparing an expectant mother for the birth of her child.

On these two pages I outline a few basic techniques that are particularly suited to pregnancy, because they increase the flexibility of the pelvic area and make it easier to adopt the upright and squatting positions that help during labour. If you find them useful, join a yoga class, or buy one of the many books on yoga during pregnancy. But check with your doctor before you try these or any other yoga exercises – gentle yoga movements are usually very beneficial for pregnant women, but in rare cases they may be inadvisable.

Start a yoga session by taking up the basic relaxation position (see pp.32-33). Concentrate on your breathing for five to ten minutes – most people don't use their full lung capacity, while some hyperventilate (breathe too rapidly) as a result of anxiety and tension. It's simple to learn to strike the correct balance: place your hands on the lower edges of your ribs with your fingers nearly touching. Inhale deeply and your fingers will move up and apart, your diaphragm will move out and down, and your stomach will rise. Hold your breath for a few seconds, then breathe out evenly – don't push, but let the air flow out, trying to ensure that all of it is expelled. Repeat this three or four times and then breathe naturally for a few minutes.

Next, stand up straight (remembering the correct posture), maintain your breathing and imagine your weight passing through your body into the floor, with your upper body free to float upwards. Then you're ready to begin to try the positions shown here.

PRACTICAL TIPS

- Ideally, plan a yoga session of between 30 minutes and an hour every day. If you don't have this much time, try to do what you can – even 15 minutes three times a week helps.

- Wear loose clothes and practise in a quiet, warm room. If you feel a little stiff in the morning, or you're tense after a hard day at work, have a warm bath before your session so that you start off relaxed and supple.

- Once in a position, try to hold it for a few minutes. Relax into it and try to empty your mind – or fix your mind on a particular object. Ignore all outward stimuli and draw your mind inwards.

- Never push, strain or exceed the limits of what is comfortable for you. Yoga is about letting go and relaxing into positions, not about forcing yourself into them.

Right Kneel on the floor with your back straight and gradually sit back on to your heels. Now gently try to separate your knees as far as they will go. Relax and hold. Then lean forward so that your elbows are on the floor. If you're still feeling comfortable, slide your hands forward in front of you.

Left Practise squatting – an excellent position for childbirth – as often as possible. Stand with your feet slightly further apart than your hips and, keeping your back straight, sink down into a squat. If your hips and knees feel stiff, use the back of a chair as a support, or bend your knees slightly, rest your hands on the floor and allow your pelvis to slide down into the position. Once you're comfortable, try holding the position while you watch television or read a book.

Right This is a good position to try in late pregnancy, when you're practising for the birth Stand as here in a good, solid position, then squeeze the muscles of the pelvic floor – as though you were trying to stop urinating – as you breathe in and relax them as you breathe out. As you exhale, imagine the baby's head pushing down on the birth canal ready to be born. Don't push down yourself, but just feel the pelvis relaxing to allow the baby to slide down.

Right This position – rather unfortunately known as the Cow pose – helps relieve tension in the neck and shoulders. Kneel or sit with a straight back, then raise one arm behind your head with the hand down your back. Bend the other arm behind your back with the hand pointing up, so that your hands are reaching for each other. Hold the position, then relax and concentrate on breathing.

Massage

As well as being extremely relaxing, a gentle massage can alleviate many minor problems that are common during pregnancy. You don't need to buy expensive aromatherapy oils, though they can be a real treat, or pay for a professional massage – but I'd thoroughly recommend one if you can afford it. The best thing to do is to persuade your partner to give you a massage: it's the most enjoyable way to relax.

Make sure that you're warm and comfortable before you start, and use pillows to give you support if necessary. If you're going to use an aromatherapy oil, check the label carefully, as some oils should not be used by pregnant women; otherwise keep it away from your stomach, or use a pure vegetable oil. Then ask your partner to concentrate on the areas in which you can feel tension or tiredness, such as the small of the back, shoulders, legs and abdomen. He should use gentle, even, smooth strokes, with the hands passed continuously and rhythmically over the skin in one direction only – this type of massage is called effleurage *(see pp.66-71)*. A word of caution, though: make sure he doesn't use deep pressure or massage over varicose veins.

Stomach massage is particularly useful during pregnancy: it can be wonderfully relaxing for you and allows

Right Using your fingers or thumbs, rub each side of the spine with small, circular movements, starting at the shoulders and working up to the base of the head. Stop the movements where the muscles meet the base of the head and press once or twice firmly, but gently, with your thumb. Repeat.

Right Place your three middle fingers in the dips between the outside of your eyes and the top of your cheek bones. Move them in a circle, clockwise, without dragging on the skin, and then pause, pressing slightly on the skin. Then press one finger gently against the skin at the point between your eyebrows.

Relaxing in Water

Whenever I want to get away from the world, I pour some oil into a hot bath, lock the bathroom door and have a long leisurely soak. It's an ideal way to relieve all your tensions and relax completely. And when you're pregnant you can rub your stomach gently, talk to your child and dream up plans for the future. Try this when you're tense – or just do it for sheer pleasure.

A visit to your local pool is less hedonistic, but swimming is also an effective way to relax and exercise: breast-stroke helps the pelvic ligaments loosen in preparation for the birth, while swimming gently on your back both relaxes you and eases back strain. The water supports your body, so your muscles don't have to strain to maintain a position and function smoothly and easily.

Below Sit up straight and rub the small of your back, working downwards on the muscles on either side of your spine.

Concentrate on the area just above the base of your spine, then move outwards across your back.

time for your partner to feel in contact with his child – and the baby will be able to feel the massage, too. Ask him to stroke your abdomen in a clockwise direction with one hand following the other, starting at the perimeter and working gradually towards the centre. And try talking to the baby at the same time: he or she will be able to hear you (*see pp.30-31*).

If your partner is not around, experiment with self-massage. You can massage your stomach as easily as he can – the only problem being that it's just not quite so nice. Massage your legs as well, starting at the ankles and working up your calves to the thighs. And remember that you can massage the back of your neck, as well as your lower spine and – most important of all – your face in order to release tensions and relieve headaches. Combined with yoga and muscle-relaxing techniques, massage will help you reduce tension and enjoy your pregnancy.

Baby's Bedroom

One of the most enjoyable aspects of preparing for a baby is deciding on how to decorate the nursery. It's often difficult to see any future after the birth – the end of pregnancy seems to be a finale, rather than the beginning of a lifetime of parenting. Creating a cosy, comfortable place for the baby before the birth can help you and your partner come to terms with the way your lives will change, and also help prepare you emotionally for the future.

Below When planning a nursery, think about what would be most stimulating for a baby. Bright colours, strong patterns and moving shapes will hold interest longer than soft shades.

Three in a bed

Many new parents find it easier for their new-born to share the main bedroom, so to start with your baby might not spend much time in the nursery. Sharing a bed is especially convenient and restful when breast feeding, as mothers only have to reach out for their babies when they want to feed them without getting up. Having your baby snuggled up next to you also helps you learn to read your baby's cues and respond to them more quickly, as well as giving the baby extra warmth and security. And many working parents

PLANNING A NURSERY

- Plan ahead. Don't save decorating until the last month of pregnancy, or you'll be too tired – and if the baby arrives a little bit early you might be stuck with a half-painted room!
- Think safety first. Cover outlets; use overhead lights or tape down cords; child-proof the windows; put a grill in front of hot radiators; use skid-proof throw rugs; make sure all the paint in the room is lead-free.
- Remember that every nursery needs a changing table, chest-of-drawers, wardrobe, shelves and lots of organizing space.
- Babies are very sensitive to light, so make sure curtains are heavy enough to keep the room dim during the day for afternoon naps.
- A mobile hung over a changing table can provide a stimulating distraction: babies like stripes and patterns better than soft pastels and are especially attracted to contrasting light and dark shapes.
- Use washable paint or wallpaper on walls, and stain-resistant carpet on the floor.

find they enjoy sharing a bed with their baby – they often feel that the extra closeness at night makes up for being apart during the day, even though their sleep might be more disturbed.

Separate rooms?

But some parents aren't comfortable about sharing a bed with their children. Don't feel guilty if you feel like this – it's perfectly natural to want some privacy. A parent who is at home with the baby all day, for instance, might well look forward to having time off at night. And many parents worry that they won't have any space left for themselves if they share a bed with their baby. It's important that your relationship as lovers continues, even though you are now parents, and many people feel inhibited about making love with a baby around. Parents also worry that the child will be unhappy sleeping elsewhere later on if they start with the baby in the bed.

There are several solutions. One is to keep the baby's crib in your bedroom. This way, each of you has your own space – and you could even consider setting up a screen around your baby. Another is to put the infant to bed in a separate nursery, and then to take the baby into bed with you after the first night feed; this way you have some private time to yourselves. It's difficult to decide which option will work best until after the birth, but do make sure that both you and your partner agree on preferences beforehand – especially if you're seriously considering having the baby sleep in your bed.

Flexibility

In my experience, it's best to be flexible about sleeping arrangements. Put your baby down for naps in the nursery and have a crib in your room for night-time; save bed-sharing for times of sickness or periods of attachment. Even babies who sleep with their parents every night learn to sleep in their own rooms once they become more independent. Establishing a night-time arrangement that suits everyone can only help your relationship with your child to build and grow over the first few years.

Above Sharing a bed with a new baby gives both parents extra time with him or her, and allows constant attention and numerous cuddles. Being so close, the parents can respond instantly to any cues – but there can be disadvantages.

III

Birth Bonding

The birth of your baby is the climax to nine months of preparation, and often to many years of expectation, too. Normally, it's a wonderful, exhilarating and emotional climax; sometimes, though the birth does not go quite the way that parents hope.

As I've said, a new-born baby's instincts are purely for survival. So this section of the book is designed to help you to bond with your new baby and start working on an approach that will make it easier for the baby to bond with you later. Instinct will be on your side – and hormones, too, for the mother – but an understanding of what is happening to the baby and parents, and what the baby's capabilities are, can make things seem much clearer.

What Happens to the Mother

For a mother, giving birth can sometimes be traumatic, but is nearly always an occasion for joy, as it is for the father, too. For both parents, parenthood becomes much more of a reality – a new baby changes your life for ever.

Childbirth is a natural event not a medical one, although it doesn't always progresses smoothly. A number of factors influence events – among the most important being the ease of the mother's own birth, later development and her genes. And research shows that that social class, wealth, illegitimacy, the mother's age and the number of her previous pregnancies all contribute to the speed and ease of labour in one way or another. A poor, young, illegitimate, unmarried mother is at high risk of a difficult labour.

Relaxed attitudes

A mother's attitude to her pregnancy and labour has a proven effect on childbirth, too. For example, anxiety is known to prolong labour and in some cases distresses the baby; and some studies have shown that a negative attitude, or excessive worry over complications, can lead to difficulties. Of course, everybody worries about these things to a certain extent, but it's a matter of degree – being overly concerned seems to increase the risk.

However, a mother has a better chance of an easy labour if she has a relaxed attitude. And there's no reason why you shouldn't – as I say, childbirth is natural, and women usually don't have any problems. (Research shows you have a head start if you have known such women, as happens in the extended family.) A positive outlook and a reliance on instinct helps the body produce more endorphins (*see pp.32-37*). As labour progresses the level of these hormones rises naturally; they reduce pain and induce a near trance-like state that lets you to go with the ebb and flow of contractions rather than fighting them.

Of course, you don't have to rely on positive attitudes and endorphins alone. A few weeks before birth, the baby's brain stimulates its adrenal glands to produce cortisone; it's the first sign that the baby is nearly ready for existence outside the womb. This has several effects: it helps the lungs to develop; and, together with glucose, released from stored fat, supplies energy to the vital organs; it also stimulates the womb to produce prostaglandins – these hormones (and oxytocin, produced by both the mother's and the baby's pituitary glands) encourage the womb to contract. Prostaglandins help to soften and ripen the neck of the womb, too – their production being stimulated by the pressure of the baby's head. The involuntary nervous system helps as well, by responding automatically to events, though it can be influenced by thought and emotion. All these systems help initiate and regulate labour, controlling the duration and frequency of the contractions.

"There is a hell"

It's impossible to explain what you'll feel during labour and delivery. I've had five babies, and each birth was different. For a mother, labour is a time of overwhelming, powerful

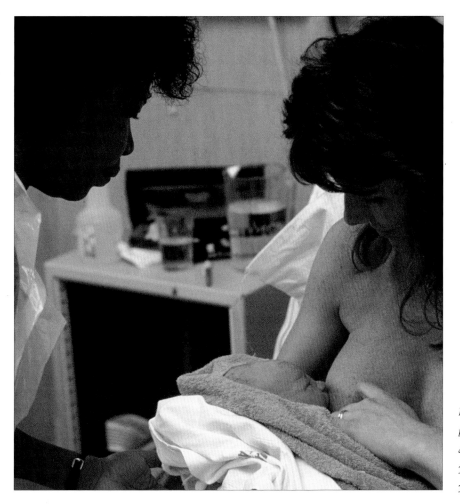

Left Most women do suffer pain during labour – but it all seems worthwhile when you hold a new-born baby in your arms.

emotions. It's much like a see-saw – up one minute with excitement and joy; down the next, feeling anxious, irritable and, above all, depressed. Some fortunate women have pain-free labours – most of us don't – and the intensity of the pain can be overwhelming at times, even to the point where you feel it's impossible to cope any longer. However, if you can relax your body and your mind completely and accept the sensations of pain, letting them wash over you, your body will cope and renew your strength and energy.

Remember, though, that childbirth is a traumatic time for your baby as well. Frédérique Leboyer, a French obstetrician, said, "There is a hell, but it's what babies go through during birth." I think this is an overstatement, but many women find sharing the pain and emotion with their babies fulfilling, because it binds them together and forms a unique bond – so much so that mothers who have pain-free labours sometimes feel cheated.

But most women rapidly forget the pain – all I remember is the joy and wonder of seeing my babies for the first time. I called myself lots of names when I went into labour, but I have never felt so complete and content as after each birth.

Skin Contact and Smell

A new-born baby has many more abilities than was once believed. New-borns can smell, taste, hear and see; their skin is extremely sensitive to temperature and touch and for an hour at least after the birth *(see pp.48-51)* they are fully conscious and alert, ready to learn about their new world.

Skin-to-skin

Provided there have been no serious complications, a mother should be able to hold her baby on her stomach immediately, either after the second stage of labour and before the umbilical cord is cut – nature has made the cord long enough for this to be possible – or, if necessary, when the baby has been checked by the doctors. This immediate contact has

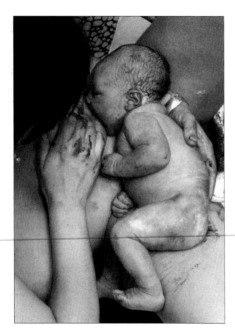

Right It's a wonderful moment for a new mother when she can see, hold and suckle her baby for the first time. And the peaceful time after the birth, when the mother relaxes, provides the ideal opportunity for bonding to start.

many benefits for both mother and baby – not only can she look into her baby's eyes, which is an important step towards forming the first bond, but skin-to-skin contact helps to keep the baby warm after the shock of birth. And while a mother is protecting her baby she can begin to explore. Research has shown that most women act in the same, instinctive way when they are first given their baby: using her fingertips first, a mother will touch and explore her baby's hands and feet and then, using her whole hand, she will stroke her baby's body with increasingly confident movements. At the same time, she will talk to her baby, trying to get his or her eyes to open – lots of mothers talk about family likenesses, such as father's ears, or grandmother's nose, though I never thought that any of mine looked like anything else but new-born babies.

This desire to hold her baby not only helps the bond, but actually makes childcare easier – the more a new-born is cuddled close the more content it becomes, because a baby needs to feel the security of touch and contact as he or she begins to learn about the new world outside the womb. Research demonstrates, too, that babies who are held and touched constantly grow, develop and settle down into organized behaviour faster than if they are seldom held and stroked *(see pp.66-71)*. Remember, though, that some babies like cuddling more than others – often, very active babies don't want the restraint of being cuddled close for too long, even though they still like the comfort of touch.

Special smells

Most mothers naturally offer their breast to the baby straight after the birth – and since childbirth has, to an extent, been reclaimed by women from the high-tech rigidity of a few decades ago, this is now generally encouraged. And the intense closeness of the moment is extremely comforting to both mother and baby. For the mother, the upheaval of birth is followed by a calm period that gives her time to realize that she really is holding her baby at last and can begin get to know him or her; and while held at the breast the baby can hear the comforting heartbeat that's familiar from the womb and learn that nibbling and sucking on the breast produces not only food, but a very special smell and taste.

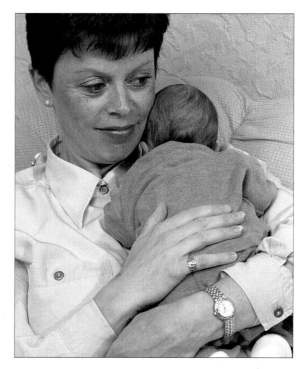

A baby's sense of taste develops in the second month of pregnancy and, as many people suspected, it has now been proved that babies prefer sweet tastes, especially that of human milk. Although our sense of smell is poor compared to that of many other animals, it's nonetheless an important sense – we can no longer scent danger, but can recognize something unusual or recall past events by a certain smell. Everyone has a unique smell and people who are related also have related smells. The sense of smell is well-developed in a new-born baby and still plays a part in its instinct for survival. Research has shown that a baby's activity – its heartbeat and breathing pattern – is altered whenever a new smell is presented, but as the smell becomes familiar the baby ceases to react. By the end of the first week a baby can distinguish his or her mother by both the smell of her body and of her milk. And this sense of smell is very powerful – if you can't feed a baby at a particular time, don't hold him or her against your breast as the baby will try to suckle your clothes and become extremely frustrated with the lack of success.

The sense of smell isn't just important because it helps a baby find food – it can also be an effective comfort. When I was busy, I used to wrap one of my night-dresses round my baby and the familiar smell provided reassurance. And in one baby-abduction case, which thankfully had a happy conclusion, the mother cuddled the baby's blanket so that the smell would remind her of her missing child. A word of warning, though – smell can be a comfort, but it can also evoke distressing memories. So if you only wear perfume when you go out, and you know your child will be upset by your absence, don't put any on until you are outside, or your child will start to whine and cling as soon as he or she smells you.

Above While you cuddle your new-born, he or she will be comforted by your smell and warmth and being able to hear the familiar beat of your heart.

The natural way

There's no doubt that the intimacy of breastfeeding helps to promote and strengthen the bond between a mother and her baby. It's the natural way to feed a baby – after all, it's why breasts exist. Breastfeeding brings mother and baby into close physical contact numerous times during the day and night, and watching each other as the baby feeds encourages a strong bond to form from the beginning.

Early bonding is not only helped by physical and visual contact, but, equally important, by the hormonal changes that occur during breastfeeding. Feeding a baby prompts the release of the mothering hormones, oxytocin and prolactin, which help to relax the mother and arouse her maternal instincts. If the baby is fed frequently and on demand, the production of these hormones will be boosted, so the mother becomes more at ease and able to cope with the demands of a new baby. These hormones play an important part in promoting the desire to care for the baby, as scientists have rather cruelly proved – rats neglect their offspring if they are deprived of these hormones.

You'll probably find breastfeeding quite difficult and painful to start with but there are many books and organizations available to help you through the initial problems. So persevere – in most cases, your efforts will be rewarded. The vast majority of women *can* breastfeed given enough encouragement and help – in Norway, for example, 99 per cent of mothers breastfeed their children. And remember that bottle feeding only developed in the mid-18th century, so it's still a comparatively new alternative. More often than not it's society that throws either mental or practical obstacles in front of new mothers, so that the natural assumption that they can and will breastfeed is undermined by the choice of an option that seems easier.

For successful breastfeeding it's vital that the mother is relaxed – tension disrupts the flow of milk to the breasts and the baby doesn't feel sufficiently safe and peaceful to feed contentedly. And if the baby picks up your tension and becomes anxious as well, the result can be painful colic and a fractious, inconsolable infant. But try as hard as you can to overcome any worries and fears that you're not doing it properly, because most breastfed babies cry less, are happier and suffer less from colic. All this makes it easier to care for the baby and cope with the demanding first few weeks.

Relaxed contentment

There are even more reasons why bottle feeding can't compete. When breastfeeding, the mother is physically connected to her baby and giving part of herself to her child, so she can be especially sensitive to the needs of the baby, making minute adjustments to her position to make feeding easier and more relaxed. And not only is the mother giving to the baby, but the baby also has some degree of control over the taking. Instead of being passively fed a bottle, when there is a tendency for the feeder to try to make the baby drink the amount of formula that the instructions state to be correct for a certain age, the baby can actively take in the amount of food that he or she wants and needs from each feed. And though formula milks are prepared very carefully, human milk is made by a mother for her baby, so its constituents are ideally suited to the digestive system and designed for the optimum development of the baby's body, and especially its brain.

A baby's feeding time is not just about nourishment. A baby soon learns that not only does feeding quench its hunger, but it's a pleasurable and comfortable experience. The

Left Learning to breastfeed your baby may take time, but it's well worth persevering. You'll find you develop a very special relationship with your child – and there are substantial physical benefits, too.

warmth of the naked breast against the skin, the familiar sound of the heartbeat and the familiar smell of the milk and body all combine to make the baby feel relaxed and content. These feelings are strengthened with each feed and give the baby a deep sense of security as he or she becomes familiar with the breasts and forms an attachment to the person to whom they belong.

Sights and Sounds

The first month or so of a new-born's life is spent adjusting to, and learning about, existence outside the womb. Babies are born with the sensory capacity to be able to begin this process immediately and do so: a new-born baby is awake for about a third of the 24-hour day, and though much of this time is taken up with feeding, plenty is left for attending to other things.

Below Within an hour of birth, a baby can focus on a human face at about the distance at which it's held when breast feeding. Babies find faces fascinating, and stare intently at them – it's a survival instinct that triggers protective urges in every family member.

Scientists used to think that infants started life with no built-in knowledge of the world, but it is now accepted that new-born babies are programmed to act in an organized way – as, indeed, they do while still in the womb (*see pp.28-29*). Researchers say that their behaviour is "unprompted, cyclic and selective", which is a complicated but shorter way of saying that the pattern of behaviour is instinctive; it has an innate rhythm (the various types of behaviour recur every three hours or so in a new-born, the interval increasing with age); and it allows for choice and preference. A baby is born with an innate predisposition for humans, for instance, and will concentrate longer on a human face and voice than anything else. This makes sense in terms of survival, because an infant who looks intently into its mother's eyes just after birth is helping her to fall in love with her child.

At birth, a baby has five different patterns of behaviour. In the order in which they occur, these are: sleeping deeply; sleeping lightly; awake; awake and excitable; and quiet and alert. Babies are most receptive to stimulation, and programmed to look for it, in the alert and quiet state. If they are in an excitable state, however, they are already being bombarded with too much stimulation or are too concerned with instinctive demands, such as that for food, to be able to pay attention to anything else. So try to develop the habit of stimulating your baby gently during quiet periods, in order to help with bonding in the future.

Focus on faces

Scientists once believed that new-borns could distinguish only light and dark at birth – I know that I keep saying what scientists once believed, but a huge amount of fascinating research has accumulated over the last 20 years. Now we know that new-born babies can focus on objects within an hour of birth at around 20-25 cm (8-10 in), and can focus as well as adults by four months. New-borns can differentiate between red, green and yellow, and prefer to look at things on their right-hand side rather than on their left. They find faces more attractive than anything else, and can see best at about the distance of a mother's face from her baby when breast feeding.

Left At first, babies find it difficult to tell the difference between a real face and a photograph. But they can tell what a proper face looks like, and soon begin to recognize individual ones.

Interestingly, babies can't tell the difference between a real face and a face in a picture, but they somehow know what a proper face looks like, despite the fact that they've never seen a human being before. In one study, new-borns were shown pictures of faces with jumbled features alongside pictures of a normal face. The correctly arranged features attracted more attention than those that were mixed-up. And at around six weeks or so, you will receive that all-important first smile when your baby looks at your face.

Babies are especially attracted to human eyes, possibly because they are drawn to patterns of light and dark, and the pupil, iris and white of the human eye provide a more interesting pattern than any other human feature. We associate eye contact with closeness – think of a couple gazing intently at each other across a table, or of the expression "look me in the eye" – and given this association, it's no wonder that many women say that they

How scientists know

I keep saying "researchers have shown", or "scientists now know" – but just how do they know? One major problem in studying new-born babies is that they can't tell us about what they see or hear and how things affect them; another is that they spend most of the time eating or sleeping, and only a only a short time in a state of quiet alertness.

But researchers have managed to overcome these obstacles, by monitoring the baby's heart rate and muscular activity: these increase with interest and excitement. Other measures of interest are the length of time an object holds a baby's attention, and how far away it can be moved before he or she stops looking at it.

When studying a baby's hearing, researchers look for behavioural changes in addition to a change in heart rate: for example, they make a judgement about whether the baby consistently becomes more active when hearing a certain sound or piece of music, or tends to quieten.

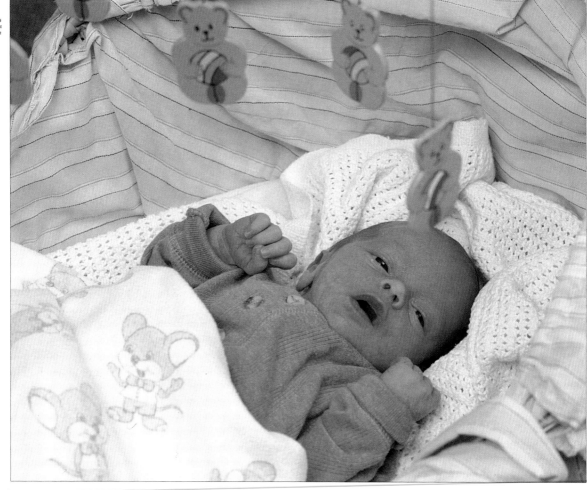

Above *Visual awareness is at its most intense during the quiet and alert state shown here. A mobile hung over a baby's crib provides a constant stimulus and will help develop co-ordination when the baby reaches out for the shapes.*

immediately felt closer to their new-born babies as soon as they were able to look into their eyes. After recovering from the trauma of birth, new-borns are usually awake and attentive for about an hour, so try to spend some time being close to your baby during this period: gazing intently into your new-born's eyes can be a wonderful and fascinating way to start bonding in earnest.

Tiny movements

Babies can hear in the womb (*see pp.30-31*), so it's not surprising that they can hear sounds and distinguish pitch and loudness from birth – though sounds are dampened for a few days by amniotic fluid from the womb, which lingers in the ears. Many studies show that new-borns not only hear passively but listen deliberately – and they seem to tune in to certain sounds more than others. For example, the sound of a heart beating has long been known to calm crying new-borns, so placing your baby on your stomach or the left side of your chest straight after birth will be a great comfort. Researchers have noticed that adults almost always cradle babies in the left arm – by instinct, I presume – regardless of whether they are left- or right-handed. This allows the baby both to listen to the heartbeat and to look at the face. And breast-feeding mothers often notice that babies quieten more quickly when offered the left breast rather than the right.

It is also known that new-born babies react in much the same way to speech as adults. Slow-motion films of adults in conversation reveal that listeners make tiny movements as an accompaniment to speakers' voices. And studies have revealed that within a day of birth – and sometimes within an hour of birth – babies start making tiny movements in time to their parents' voices. Within several days after birth, babies start to associate sights with sounds, and try to look towards noises that are especially startling or pleasing.

New-borns are very good imitators, too. Imitation seems to be another inborn response, though it fades as the baby matures. If you catch your new-born baby's attention and start to open and close your mouth, put out your tongue or blink rapidly, your baby will imitate you. This can be a delight to new parents, who realize their baby is interacting, and not just reacting to voice and movement. And imitation is another way of establishing communication, which is important for bonding as well as for development.

Below Most mothers – and fathers, too – instinctively hold a baby with its head to the left side of the body. That means the baby can hear the comforting sound of a heartbeat, and look into the adult's face.

All the above demonstrates that babies are programmed to tune in to sights and sounds from birth – indicating that they are predisposed to be social creatures and interact with anyone who provides stimulation. This makes getting to know your baby, recognizing his or her character and forming a bond considerably easier.

Developing associations

As your baby grows, he or she will soon learn to link familiar sights with familiar sounds. In one study, two-week-old babies were shown to associate the sound of their mothers' voices with their faces. Typically, a baby was very attracted to its mother's face and voice, and became confused and disturbed if another woman's face was being watched while its mother's voice could be heard.

Hearing will also become more significant as the baby grows older. New-born babies are attracted by pleasant sounds and turn away from loud, unattractive noises. But soon they begin to associate the sound of your voice with other pleasant sensations, such as food and warmth. A crying baby knows that the approach of footsteps means the alleviation of hunger and discomfort, and often learns to settle before you appear. Then, at about three months, babies start to understand routines: a bored, fractious baby may hear you opening a closet to get a jacket, for example, and see you putting on a baby sling or getting out a push chair, and will recognize this as a routine that has to be endured before you go out together for a walk; as a result, he or she will stop being fractious and quieten down expectantly.

Birth in Other Cultures

A s far as western obstetrics (the medical specialty concerned with pregnancy and childbirth) is concerned, the story of the 20th century has been one of continual technological advance. The result has been a drastic reduction in the number mothers and babies dying in childbirth, and an easing of the pain of labour.

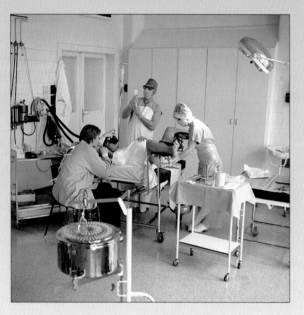

Obviously, this has been a good thing. But, unfortunately, the technological advances went hand-in-hand with increasingly authoritarian and interventionist medical attitudes. Women were routinely anaesthetized during labour and forced to adopt the "stranded beetle" position – so much so that in 1942, Grantly Dick-Read, a British obstetrician, commented: "an offspring is produced by a magician from a paralyzed birth canal". Pregnancy was viewed and treated as an illness, and the birth process handled with impersonal, invasive and often unnecessary procedures. The whole business, which made a mother feel almost irrelevant, was hardly good for bonding.

In the late 1960s, though, a reaction began to set in. The emphasis began to swing towards making childbirth a personal and fulfilling experience; in fact, it was a reversion to traditional methods, with a mother's preferences being respected and intervention reduced.

Above *Things are much better than they were, but many mothers still find that a high-tech birth in hospital detracts from the emotion and satisfaction of birth. But most mothers agree that the presence of medical staff and equipment can be very reassuring if things start to go wrong.*

The natural way

Even so, there's a long way to go before having a baby in western society is the same natural process as in non-industrialized cultures. In such cultures, babies are delivered at the mother's home or in a special birthing hut, often with a number of other women in attendance to give help and support, and in an atmosphere of celebration and ceremony. The main helper is usually an experienced older woman, rather than a midwife with formal training and qualifications. Often this woman plays a larger role than the western midwife: the traditional Jamaican *nana*, for instance, visits the mother on numerous occasions during the pregnancy to care for her and to give advice and stays at the mother's home for a few days after the birth to look after her.

Women in traditional societies are generally allowed much more freedom of movement during labour, too. It is very common for women in western hospitals to stay flat on their backs and hooked up to monitors throughout labour. While these women are almost always given drugs to help them manage the pain of labour, traditional methods are much less complicated. For example, a Jamaican *nana* will massage and comfort the mother, while in parts of Guatemala pain relief involves a herbal sweat bath as well as massage.

After the birth, the mother and her baby are allowed, indeed expected, to stay together – the baby isn't immediately whisked away as in many modern hospitals. This, of course, allows for the vital mother-child bonding *(see pp.42-43)* to take place quickly and calmly. The mother is allowed to deliver the placenta (the afterbirth) naturally, without fuss and without drugs being administered to speed up the process. If it's taking too long, she is usually asked to blow into a bottle, which encourages the placenta to separate from the wall of the womb. And the mother is encouraged to start breastfeeding immediately, which also helps to expel the placenta.

Unclean

It would be silly to pretend, of course, that everything about approaches to childbirth in a traditional society are wonderful. They're not – and I would certainly always want to have access to sophisticated medical technology if something went wrong, as sometimes it does; I've had occasion to be grateful to modern obstetric science myself. And sometimes traditional childbirth involves a number of customs that western mothers would find unacceptable. In many societies there is still a belief that a mother and her new-born baby are unclean, and in extreme cases they are isolated from men for a set period.

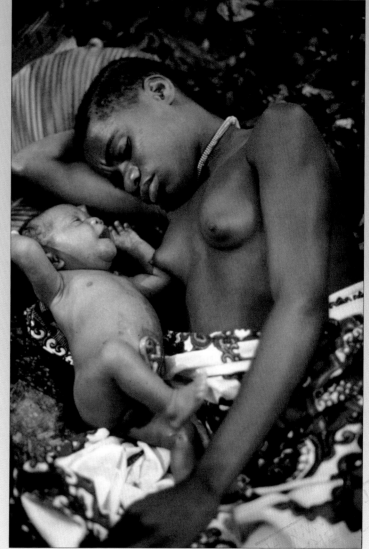

Obviously, this hardly promotes bonding with the father. On the other hand, it does give the mother time to rest and recover – and a period of rest and quiet is desirable after any birth. Bedouin women, for example, stay at home for 40 days after childbirth. During this time, they are not supposed to do any cooking or housework. They rest, eat well and visit other female relatives or companions and receive lots of care, support and advice. It sounds tempting – especially when a western mother is often discharged from hospital after a 48-hour stay to fend for herself, sometimes without any support from friends and relatives, and can find it hard extremely hard to feel sufficiently rested, calm, happy and eager to bond with her new baby.

Above The traditional approach to birth emphasizes warmth, closeness and quiet for mother and baby to get to know each other.

Bonding After a Difficult Birth

The first few moments and hours after birth are very important for the development of a bond between a mother and her child *(see pp.42-51)*. In an ideal world, of course, a relationship would start to form during this time, but it is neither absolutely essential nor always possible in practical terms that it should do so. But the fact that a mother and her new-born baby are not able to be together immediately after the birth does not preclude strong bonding in the future.

There are a number of reasons why mothers may not be able to form an immediate attachment to their babies. Sometimes, unfortunately, the mother thinks that her baby is just not the perfect one that she expected – the baby may have a handicap, or may simply not be of the desired sex. But generally the problem is caused by the length and severity of labour – even though most women don't experience any serious difficulties during it. If, for example, a mother is given pain-killing drugs during labour, she may well still be under their influence for some time afterwards. Even without drugs or medical intervention, an extremely long, but otherwise uneventful labour can leave a mother drained, both physically and emotionally. She may feel great relief that the labour is over, but be too exhausted to feel unable to feel any joy at the sight and sound of her new baby.

Sympathetic care

Sometimes medical intervention is necessary to deliver the baby safely and protect the mother, and this may involve a general anaesthetic when a caesarian operation is needed. Anyone who has a general anaesthetic is likely to feel depressed for about three to four

Right Don't worry if you are too exhausted after a difficult labour to react joyfully to your new-born. Wait until you are fully rested before you begin bonding.

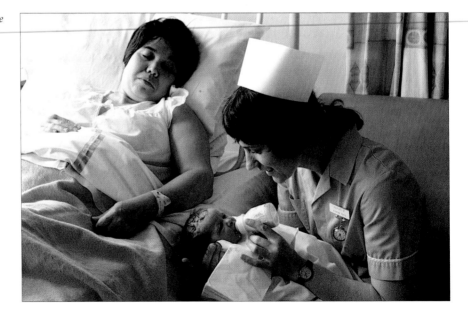

days after the operation – and all mothers tend to feel low after the birth because of the hormonal changes that are taking place *(see pp.42-43)*. Taken together, these difficulties mean that women who have had a caesarian operation are very likely to feel quite severely depressed. And abdominal discomfort, wind and indigestion, which often follow this operation, hardly help. Such mothers need very sympathetic care from all concerned – hospital staff, partners, relations, other children, friends – and, most importantly, they need enough time to recover. No woman who has had a caesarian should have to care for her baby full time until ready to do so. A small amount of positive, loving contact between mother and baby is better for both than constant contact when the mother may feel that looking after her baby is sheer drudgery.

Scrawny and red

A few new-borns need special care in an incubator or a special-care unit because they are ill, premature or have a low birth-weight. In such cases, the birth often arouses a mass of conflicting emotions and feelings in the parents.

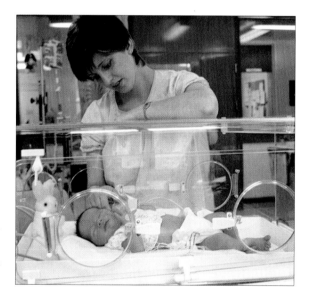

Premature babies, in particular, give rise to special problems with bonding. Often the parents are not psychologically prepared for the birth, and the mother may suffer feelings of guilt, believing that it is her fault that the baby was born too early. And very small premature babies bear little resemblance to the stereotype of a clean, bouncing new-born; in fact, their appearance can be very off-putting. They are scrawny, red and often covered all over with soft downy hair. Under these circumstances, with minimal contact between parents and baby, and no possibility of breastfeeding, it's not surprising if the parents don't feel an instantaneous surge of love for their new-born, because other emotions usually get in the way. It takes a little time for the parents to adjust to the situation and begin to feel that their baby really is wonderful and special.

Above If your baby is in an incubator, spend as much time together as you can. Touch and stroke, and a bond will begin to form.

There are ways to shorten this time, however. First and foremost, try not to worry about how you feel, but spend as much time with your baby as you can, so that you become used to each other. Touch and stroke your baby as much as possible *(see pp.66-71)*, even when the baby is in an incubator, and trace his or her face, nose and eyes with your fingers.

Back home, let your new-born's fingers move over your face so he or she can learn about you. Wear your baby *(see pp.60-65)* whenever possible – doing so helps a premature baby gain weight; work on eye contact, either when you're holding your child or lying down together side by side. Hold your baby close, so that he or she can smell you and be comforted by your body warmth. If possible, sleep with your baby near you – or in your bed *(see pp.38-39)*. And if you still have problems, seek advice from a professional. Above all, though, let time help to heal the wounds and forge the bonds.

The First Few Days at Home

I didn't have any of my babies at home, and for most mothers today it still isn't possible or practical to do so – interestingly, though, 50 per cent of all Dutch babies are delivered at home, yet the mortality rate in Holland is lower than in both Britain and America. It must be wonderful to have your baby in your own bed, surrounded by familiar things – and, of course, it avoids the abrupt break in routine that comes when you leave hospital.

In a hospital, too, there are trained, experienced people to help you and answer all your queries; meals arrive at set times, and all you have to do care for your baby and try to rest. At home, a mother has to cope with a tiny, helpless and demanding scrap of humanity 24 hours a day, and probably doesn't feel at all confident about her ability to handle the situation. And fathers often seem to think that women are natural mothers, coping by instinct – unless they have been reminded of the reality. But there are ways of making that first day at home a more welcoming and relaxing experience.

A helping hand

A new-born baby needs warmth, peace and quiet and food. A new mother needs much the same, partly in order to get over the physical strain of the birth, and partly so that she can breastfeed effectively (see pp.44-47). And the best way to ensure that both mother and baby are happy and in a position to bond is to make sure there's someone at home to help you for the first few days – your partner, your mother, your partner's mother, or a close friend (it's obviously helpful, though it's far from essential, if the person you choose has some experience with new-born babies).

Your helper's prime function should be to take over the running of the household and the chores, leaving you free to relax following the birth, to look after your baby and get to know him or her. Don't let anyone take over caring for your baby, though, however confident and capable he or she might be – you only acquire confidence in your abilities through practice, not by watching someone else. The first few days at home should be for you and your baby to settle down together; think of anything else as secondary. Leave the rest to someone else, or, if there's no one else, forget about it until later. Your baby won't mind if you forget to brush your hair, stay in bed until midday, or don't change into smart clothes for visitors – and you shouldn't mind either.

Visitors, by the way, can be a major stumbling block. The trouble is that, reasonably enough, they want to see your new baby, but he or she won't want to see them – or, rather, won't want to be bothered with all the fuss and disturbance that visitors inevitably cause. Try to resist the temptation to show your new baby to all and sundry, and keep callers to a bare minimum for the first few days. If people insist on calling, ask your helper to entertain them, and make sure that you keep the visits as short as possible. Don't hurry a feed if others are around – in fact, it's best to breastfeed your baby in quiet and private surroundings until you get used to the technique.

Enjoying your baby

While a new mother is resting, relaxing and recovering, both she and her partner have an opportunity to enjoy their baby, to start to form a relationship with a unique individual and to form bonds. After all the months of waiting, you will now be able to see the reaction to sounds that have become familiar during pregnancy, such as your voice and music (*see pp.30-31*). So talk as you feed, change, bathe and cuddle your baby – making sure that both you and your partner are involved in these activities; play the same soft, relaxing music as before on your stereo and lull him or her to sleep with familiar lullabies.

As you both come to know your child as a person, with individual quirks, foibles and characteristics, you'll soon find it difficult, if not impossible, to believe that there was a time when he or she wasn't part of your lives.

Left Rest and relaxation are the most vital ingredients for your first days at home with your new baby. Try to find someone to help you during this time – someone who is a calming influence, who can deal with routine chores and give you the support you need while you recover from the birth – and adjust to the fact that there is a new and very important person in your life.

IV

THE FIRST YEAR

YOU'LL SPEND the first few months after the birth
adjusting to the changes that a new baby makes to
your household. But try to spend as much time
with your baby as you can, so that
you learn to feel relaxed and happy
with each other and develop the
skill of reading your baby's cues – it
doesn't always happen as easily as
you might think.

Try to include other members of the
family in the baby's routine from the
start. Not only is making multiple
bonds important for your baby, but you'll be
glad of the extra help. The first year with your
new baby will speed by and he or she will
change and develop every day. So make sure
that you take good care of yourself and your
partner as well as your baby, to ensure that you
can both enjoy this time to the full.

Babywearing

In most non-industrialized cultures, babies have always been "worn" by their mothers – whether in a sling, a cradleboard or a similar device. Baby and mother are often regarded as one unit in such cultures, not only during pregnancy but throughout infancy – for instance, the Ndembu tribe, of Zambia, calls the cloth that attaches the baby to the mother's back the "placenta".

Below One advantage that babywearing slings have over other carriers is that they allow discreet breast feeding whenever necessary.

Over the last 20 years, babywearing has also become popular in western cultures – and understandably so, because it has a number of advantages. On the practical side, babywearing is much more convenient when you're out and about than carrying the baby in your arms or using a stroller, and parents can have their hands free to attend to household chores or other children, while giving a baby comfort and security. Babywearing is ideal for breast feeding, too – in fact, in agricultural societies, where milk substitutes are not available and women work in the fields all day, it's essential. In western societies, babywearing allows a baby to feed at will without interfering with the mother's daily routine, and can be done discreetly, if you chose a sling. Babies who have trouble settling down for long feeds tend to suck for longer when the mother feeds and walks at the same time Needless to say, a sling is especially effective with babies who have sucking problems: the comfort of the skin and mother's movements relax the baby's whole body, including the sucking muscles, making feeding easier. And it's a great help if you don't have to stop everything every 20 minutes or so for a quick feed; you're much more likely to see your baby as a joy rather than a burden if you don't feel your freedom is being restricted. Your baby will sense that you genuinely enjoy your time together, and will also feel loved and appreciated.

Relaxed interaction

The practical advantages are considerable, but babywearing can also help promote the all-important bond. If a baby is carried, instead of left in a baby seat or playpen, mother and baby cannot help but interact more. And wearing a new-born in a semi-upright position also increases the amount of time the baby is alert and capable of interaction, as very young infants become drowsy when lying on their backs. You can also respond to your baby's cues more quickly if your baby is with you, rather than in a crib on the other side of the room. Out of doors, you can maintain eye contact with your baby and watch his or her reactions to the world going by much more easily when using a baby carrier than a stroller.

There are specific advantages for the mother, as well. A woman's mothering hormones *(see pp.42-43)* are stimulated by close contact with her infant. These hormones have a calming, relaxing effect, which fades after about half an hour if the mother and baby are separated. But the production of the hormones is stimulated continuously by babywearing, so their effect persists. This may explain why some research has indicated that mothers who wear their babies frequently are much less likely to suffer the ordeal of post-natal depression.

Quiet and alert

Babywearing can also benefit an infant physically, because constant close contact helps to control breathing and movements, which increases the amount of time during which a baby is quiet and alert, rather than restless and fussy *(see pp.48-51)*. On the surface, this may seem unlikely, but studies have shown that a baby moves its limbs less the more it hears its mother's voice; a baby in a sling hears its mother constantly and only rarely produces the erratic, jerky, limb movements characteristic of new-borns. The constant motion a carried baby experiences also helps develop the vestibular apparatus of the inner ear, which gives the brain information about the body's position in relation to its surroundings and provides the sense of balance.

Right Baby carriers rather than strollers allow eye contact to be maintained, enabling a mother to respond quickly to cues and watch her baby's reaction.

SAFETY WATCHPOINTS

- Buy your baby carrier from a well-known, trusted manufacturer.
- Support your baby with your hands while you are getting used to the carrier, especially if he or she starts to squirm.
- Make sure the carrier is fastened correctly, and that it is snug enough to support your baby firmly.
- Avoid making any sudden movements, especially twisting or lunging.
- If you are wearing an older baby or toddler, keep an eye on what may be in reach. Avoid using knives or carrying hot liquids.
- Check with your doctor before wearing a heavy toddler if you have back problems. If you need to pick something up while wearing your baby, try to bend at the knees, keeping your back straight.

Opposite *Young children love to feel part of what's going on: if they are too young to carry a new-born baby, or not sufficiently strong, make them a toy sling for a favourite teddy bear or doll.*

Sharing the wearing

Other members of the family can also take advantage of the benefits of babywearing. Fathers can spend more time interacting and promote bonding by wearing their babies – and give their partners a rest while they're doing it. Your other children can be involved as well: in many non-industrialized societies, older brothers and sisters take care of younger ones by wearing them, and both boys and girls have babies strapped to their backs almost as soon as they can walk properly. This gives the parents a break and also helps prepare the older children for parenthood. If you have older children, give them a chance to get closer to their little brother or sister by letting them do some babywearing. And if your children are still too young to carry an infant, make a sling so that they can carry a teddy bear or doll – children love to imitate adults, and this will help them feel part of what is going on.

Remember, too, that the comfort and familiarity of a sling can also help babies who are afraid of strangers. Often there will be far less fretting if a baby is transferred from one person to another while still in a carrier, because the familiarity of the carrier and the position in which the baby is held is comforting and provides continuing security.

Fussy and dependent?

Right *Some babies prefer a forward-facing position, because it gives a better view of what's happening around them.*

Some parents feel that there is something rather wet about babywearing, and worry that their baby will be spoilt and grow up to be fussy and dependent. In fact, studies have shown that babies who are carried actually cry less than babies who are not – and that means they are bonding better and becoming slowly less dependent on their parents. In cultures in which babywearing is

Changing positions

Not all babies enjoy being worn for long periods of time, so pay attention to your baby's cues and experiment with different types of carrying positions. It's best to hold a new-born in a cradle position, or snuggled up to your body. Once your baby gets stronger and more co-ordinated, though, he or she may enjoy the stimulation of looking out at the world.

Try carrying your child on your hip, or in a forward-facing position – one of my children loved this because she could watch what I was doing and look at what was going on around her, but still had the security of being held snugly against me. The position your baby prefers will depend upon his or her mood: an anxious or upset child may prefer a closer, more restrictive hold; while one who is peaceful and content may want to take part in what you are doing.

commonplace, the amount of time a baby spends crying every day is measured in minutes, while in western cultures it's measured in hours. This is probably because mothers who carry their babies are able to respond to cues before their babies feel the need to start crying. And the less time a baby spends fussing, the more both mother and baby enjoy their time together. Another reason that babies who are worn cry less is that the baby finds being this way of being carried reminiscent of life in the womb; he or she is comforted by the familiar rhythm of the mother's walk, and can hear her heartbeat when snuggled up close to her body.

Of course there comes a time when a child grows out of babywearing. The process can be a stop-start affair, though. For a while the child may well become rather anxious and demand to be carried again. The important thing is to be sensitive about what is happening, and react positively to what is needed – carrying him or her again if necessary – and soon your child will feel just as happy and secure when not being carried. Babywearing doesn't teach children dependency, just that their mother's or father's arms are always available when needed.

Below left A sturdy backpack-type carrier is ideal for longer outings. The baby is very secure, and the framework reduces the strain on parents' backs they are wearing their bay for any length of time.

Sleeping problems

As you might expect, there is a downside to babywearing: some children feel so snug and secure while sleeping in a baby carrier that they find it difficult or impossible to sleep anywhere else. Some experts feel that babywearing encourages babies to sleep during the day instead of at night; others disagree, claiming that a baby will take short naps in the carrier during the day and save longer sleep periods for night-time. Because babywearing is fairly new to western society, and because all babies are different, it is difficult to say which school of thought is correct. But the benefits of babywearing far outweigh this one drawback, so at least try the technique and see how you get on – if necessary, wait until your child falls asleep in the carrier before putting put him or her down for longer naps or down for the night.

Opposite left This sling is especially convenient because it allows you to move your baby into different positions, depending on his or her mood and state of wakefulness.

Below This American-style sling is reminiscent of ones used in non-industrialized cultures. Once you become used to the lack of a frame, both you and your baby will find this type of sling very comfortable – it is fairly easy to adjust to different positions, depending on your baby's preferences.

Baby Massage

PREPARATION

- Take off rings and jewellery, wash your hands and make sure your nails are short.
- Make sure the room is warm, quiet and softly lit.
- Use baby massage oil, almond or light vegetable oil. Baby Oil is not suitable.
- Put a nappy under your baby's bottom, and a nappy over a boy's penis – I used an egg cup – to avoid being squirted in the eye during the course of the massage.

Massage – from the Arabic word *masah*, meaning "to stroke with the hand" – is as old as the hills. Humans have always had an instinct to cuddle babies and hug, but in the West instinct is often overridden by embarrassment. And that's a pity, because research shows that a lack of close, regular physical contact holds back a baby's ability to relate to others and relax with them.

Other research has demonstrated the positive side of baby massage beyond doubt: it can help babies, toddlers and children to develop body image – a mental picture of the body, its components and boundaries. A positive and realistic body image can help to reduce anxiety and increase physical ability and self-esteem in later life. Studies have also shown that babies massaged regularly from birth often gain weight faster than others – possibly because massage stimulates the production of growth hormones – and are less fretful and more socially alert.

There is nothing very difficult about massaging your baby – essentially the movements are gentler versions of those used on adults. Start with a facial massage so that your face can be seen, to relax the baby and maximize interaction. Then enjoy the warmth, closeness and affection of baby massage. And see your baby enjoy it, too.

Acupressure points for headaches: the dip just outside the outer edge of each eye; at the top of the nose between the eyebrows; the dips where the cheekbones meet the ears.

Acupressure point for pain: immediately beneath the nose, in the centre.

Acupressure point for wind: a thumb's breadth to the right and left of the navel.

Acupressure point for eczema: just above the web between the big toe and the first toe.

Acupressure point for insomnia: pinch the ear lobe gently.

Acupressure point for teething pain: just above the web between the thumb and the first finger.

FACIAL MASSAGE

Stroke the face and head in circular or straight movements. Any movement that the baby enjoys is fine, but take special care around the eyes – if the baby does not like its eyes being covered, try playing peekaboo games – and over the fontanelles (the bones of the skull that have yet to fuse together) in a new-born.

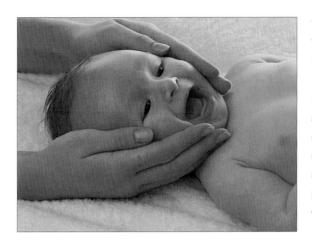

EFFLEURAGE

This is the rather pompous medical word for "stroking" – the massage movement that is most often used with babies and toddlers. Use your fingers and thumbs to stroke small areas, such as the face, hands and feet, rather than the whole palm. If your baby doesn't enjoy what you're doing, stop.

◁ *1. Stroke from the chin up the sides of the face and to the centre of the forehead. Always make sure the massage is gentle and rhythmic.*

▷ *2. With your thumbs together in the centre of the forehead, stroke across the forehead and down, ending with your hands behind the baby's ears.*

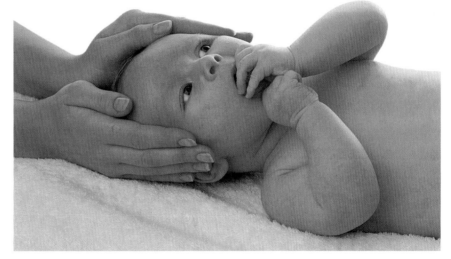

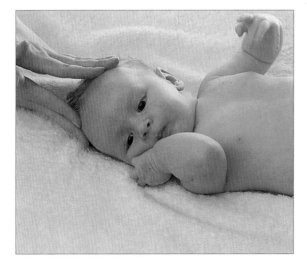

◁ *3. Gently massage the head with your fingers as if you were shampooing the hair – some babies are afraid of having their hair washed, and this movement will help take any fear out of bath time.*

PRESSURE POINTS

Apply gentle but steady pressure for about 20 seconds to the acupressure points shown in the illustration opposite, which are used in Eastern massage. If your baby enjoys this, repeat two or three times.

BACK MASSAGE

Most people love a back massage and babies are no exception, so it's a good idea to try back massage first if your baby doesn't enjoy any other type. Babies seem to divide into two groups from birth: some babies can't get enough cuddles and massages; others don't seem to like much physical contact. In fact, it is not so much that the latter group dislikes being touched as that it is averse to any feeling of restraint; of being passive rather than active. A back massage is particularly suitable for this type of baby and you will quickly get used to the squirming and kicking.

▷ *1. Put your naked baby face down on a warm towel. Check that your hands are warm, then run them the spine and down each side of the back in a circular, rhythmic movement. Next, circle around the shoulder blades with your thumbs; then squeeze the fleshy parts in between the blades gently and follow up the spine through to the shoulders. Make all the movements smooth and fluid and repeat each of them four to five times.*

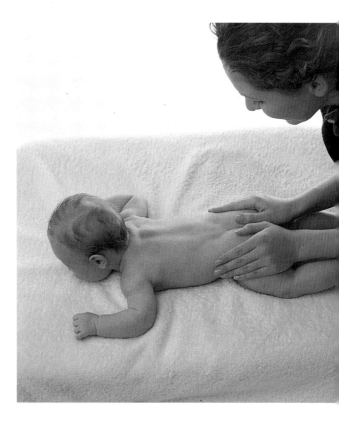

◁ *2. Grip the flesh on each side of the spine gently with your fingers, lift it and then let go – moving from top to bottom of the spine. Next, rake gently down the spine with your finger tips (don't do this if you have long nails). Then repeat the whole process in the opposite direction.*

▷ *3. Make sure that there's a towel under your baby, because this technique might make him or her pee. Knead the flesh of the buttocks, then use firm, circular, stroking movements at the top of the bottom, round the outsides and up the middle. Try patting and pinching gently. Move fluidly down to the thighs and continue on the fleshy areas there.*

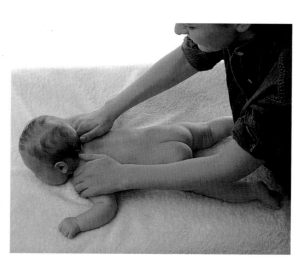

PETTRISAGE

This is the technique of rolling, squeezing and kneading flesh – a restrained version of what you would do with a ball of dough. Use it on the fleshy parts of the body, such as the buttocks and thighs. Move the palms of your hands in circular movements or knead the flesh with your fingers and thumbs.

MASSAGING ARMS AND LEGS

▷ *1. Hold up your baby's arm or leg and stroke down to the end in gentle flowing movements. Continue with the other limbs.*

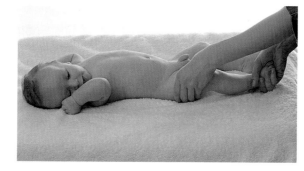

▽ *3. Open your baby's hand and massage the palm with circular movements of your thumb, then stroke the back of the hand. Uncurl the fingers and gently squeeze and rotate each finger, before giving it a gentle pull.*

▽ *2. Hold each foot and massage its front and back, as with the hand. Take the ankle joint through all its movements. Finally, squeeze and pull each toe separately.*

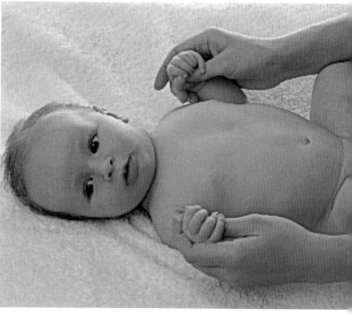

FRONT MASSAGE

▷ *1. Lie your baby face up on a warm towel and stroke up and down the body from the top of the thighs to the shoulder muscles using a gliding movement. Use both hands, moving them in the same direction at first; then alternate them, with one hand going up and the other down. Finally, stroke across the body from side to side.*

TAPOTEMENT

A massage technique involving pinching, pummelling, cupping and flicking – though it's much less aggressive than this sounds. Flick with the outside edge of your hands in a light chopping motion – practise on your partner or a cushion first. Cupping is self-explanatory, though you give the technique rhythm by cupping each hand alternately. All tapotement movements should be rhythmical, gradually increasing in pressure if your baby enjoys it. Don't use this technique on bony parts of the body: it's only suitable for fleshy areas.

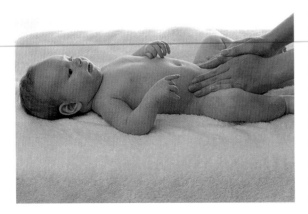

△ *2. Massage the stomach and abdomen using smooth, circular movements going clockwise, with one hand following the other. Be* *warned – such movements can help relieve pain when a baby suffers from colic, but they can also stimulate the bladder.*

▽ 3. Continue the massage up the chest, using the same smooth strokes and circular movements. There are no rules in baby massage, provided you are gentle and the baby is happy - it is the physical contact that is important for relaxation and development.

WHAT MASSAGE CAN DO

- The physical contact, touching and cuddling involved in massage promotes bonding.
- Research shows that premature babies who are massaged from birth gain weight more quickly than those who are not, and that older babies who are massaged develop physically and grow faster as well. This may be because touch increases the levels of the hormone that controls growth, and also the digestive hormones.
- Massage triggers the release of endorphins, the hormones that aid relaxation, so babies become less agitated and sleep better after a massage.
- Some studies have suggested that massage promotes the development of myelin – this is an insulating material, laid down around every nerve as a baby matures, that allows nerve impulses to travel faster. So the neurological development of a baby who is massaged frequently may speed up.
- Massage helps babies to develop proprioception – an awareness of the relation of individual parts of the body to the whole, and awareness of the entire body to its position in relation to the outside world; in short, a mental image of ourselves.

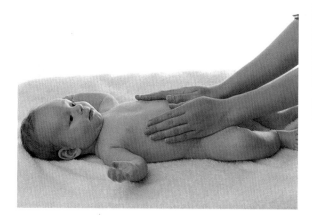

◁ 4. Finish the massage with sweeping movements up to the top of the shoulders, either moving your hands in towards the neck or outwards over both shoulders. Be careful not to catch your fingernails on the skin as you go over the shoulders.

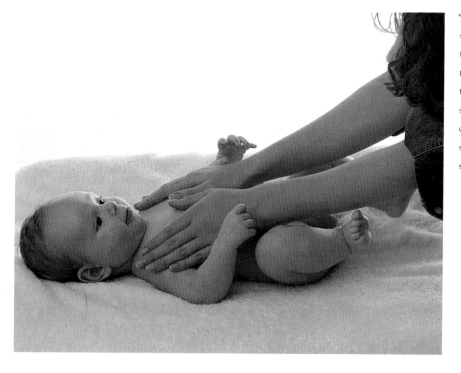

Coping with Post-baby Blues

Above Post-baby blues can add to the problems and upheavals following a birth; it's important that both partners understand the condition and realize that is will pass shortly.

About half of all mothers feel depressed after giving birth: they cry without any apparent reason, and suffer from lethargy, insomnia, anxiety and loss of appetite. Collectively known as the "post-baby blues", these symptoms usually appear three or four days after the birth, and subside without any treatment in two weeks with understanding and support from close family members.

Nevertheless, the blues can be both depressing and scaring for mothers, especially when partners and relatives, thrilled by the new baby, respond with forced sympathy and an unspoken "pull yourself together". The first thing to remember is that post-baby blues are completely different from post-natal depression, which is a much more serious and debilitating condition, requiring medical attention (*see Box*).

Second, it is important for both parents to appreciate that the causes of post-baby blues are believed to physical in origin as well as psychological. During pregnancy, the blood levels of the hormones progesterone and oestrogen become very high, then drop rapidly after the baby is born. In addition, the levels of oxytocin (the hormone that stimulates the flow of milk from the breasts) rise suddenly when proper milk production starts, about three to five days after the birth. And these abrupt physiological changes can trigger the post-baby blues in some women.

The sudden psychological changes a mother experiences may also play a part. Many women spend the nine months of pregnancy planning for and thinking about the birth. If it doesn't go according to plan, the resulting disappointment can be difficult to overcome. Some expect to bond with their babies instantly, and feel guilty when they don't; rigid hospital routines can make mothers feel inadequate, too, and distance them from their

Post-natal depression

Post-natal depression is a psychological condition that occurs after about 10 per cent of all births, and requires medical attention. It can take several weeks to surface, and can last for months or even years, with symptoms often worsening during menstruation. Women who suffer from post-natal depression can have a variety of symptoms, including loss of energy and enthusiasm, insomnia, weight loss, panic attacks, loss of concentration and memory, irritability, and a general feeling of inability to cope. If you think you or your partner may be a sufferer, consult your doctor immediately.

No-one knows why some women only suffer a day or two of the blues and others develop post-natal depression, though it seems that a genetic factor is involved – women with mothers or identical twin sisters who have developed from post-natal depression are more likely to be sufferers themselves. On very rare occasions, depression can develop into a psychosis – that is, a severe mental illness in which a mother loses touch with reality and becomes dangerous both to herself and to her baby. It is essential that a mother suffering from post-natal depression or psychosis seeks medical advice, because a seriously depressed woman doesn't have the capacity to care for herself, let alone a demanding new-born, and it is completely impossible for a healthy bond to grow between mother and baby.

Left Fathers can play a
positive role when a mother
has the post-baby blues by
fending off visitors and
caring for the child while the
mother rests.

babies. And mothers who are inexperienced with babies sometimes panic when they get
home and have no nurses or doctors to ask for help and advice. Generally, though, women
who don't start to form a bond with their babies before they leave hospital are more likely
to get the blues once they get home.

The way forward

The best way to cope with post-baby blues and move forward is to recognize the condition
for what it is, work out your own feelings and work through them – I know that's easy to
say, but it's the only solution. It's helpful, too, if both parents talk about the possibility of
post-baby blues before the birth, so that the mother gets the support and help she needs as
soon as she begins to feel depressed; telling your partner to pull herself together will only
make her feel guilty and may well prolong the problem. Often all a mother needs is to rest
in bed for a couple of days and for an understanding partner to fend off visitors.

One of the best ways to speed recovery from the blues is to spend as much time as
possible with your baby. Physical contact stimulates production of the mothering
hormones (*see pp.42-43*), which have a relaxing effect and which may alleviate the
anxiety that some new mothers feel. If a mother concentrates on her baby, and is freed
from other worries by supportive family members, the baby alone will often have a
therapeutic effect. As the bond between mother and baby begins to form, she will enjoy
the baby more and feel less anxious and upset.

Music and Movement

In every culture, music helps form bonds and reinforce relationships – think of the way you react to your national anthem, or use music to change your mood. And music is important for a baby, too. As I said earlier (*see pp.30-31*), research demonstrates that babies react to music even during life in the womb: tests have shown that an unborn baby becomes more alert and its heartbeat changes when listening to a tune that has become familiar during the course of pregnancy.

After a baby is born, music takes on an added importance. From the first week, your baby can distinguish one sound from another (medical textbooks of the 1950s had it that babies were deaf for the first two weeks) – and to a baby the most important sound of all is that of a human voice. So the use of music, together with the distinctively different tones of the voices of you and your partner, can be a vital help to the process of bonding: music and movement can stimulate your baby both physically and mentally, and promote increased closeness through a shared activity. (Interestingly, music therapy is recommended quite commonly by doctors nowadays to help treat children who suffer from depression and a lack of social skills.)

But how can you put the theory into practice? Not by simply playing music. The secret lies in the three "Rs": in this case, Repetition, Rhythm and Rhyme. Involve your baby by fitting actions to song, as happens in many traditional nursery rhymes. Help your baby learn the various nuances of your voice by changing tones and pitch, and, above all, encourage him or her to become involved in the fun.

Opposite Babies love to feel that they are helping to make a noise – and especially one that sounds pleasant and tuneful. If you have a piano – or any musical instrument, for that matter – play to your baby and let him or her experiment: even if the result sounds horrible to you. If not, it's easy to use an old biscuit tin as a makeshift drum or even to blow through a comb covered in lavatory paper.

Bouncing baby

It's good for your baby to feel absolutely secure with you in a physical, as well as a mental sense – so that there's no fear of falling and your baby always feels safe; rough and tumble also helps develop a sense of spatial awareness.

One way to promote this is by bouncing and dancing to the rhythm of a song or nursery rhyme – slowly at first, with lots of cuddles, then building up to more vigorous and stimulating movements. But slow down if your baby seems at all anxious.

The Extended Family

I've said before that bonding takes place much more naturally in communities in which the extended family – by which I mean relations other than mother, father and siblings – is at hand *(see pp.22-23)*, and I've also talked about the importance of multiple bonds *(see pp.10-13)*. If you are lucky enough to have members of your extended family living nearby, make the most of it, because they provide an ideal opportunity for your child to form multiple bonds. And each bond will have its own value: grandparents, for example, can give a sense of family history and continuity; cousins may be the first children to play with your child and help teach him or her social skills; aunts and uncles may have different ways of bringing up children.

Traditional attachments

In non-industrial cultures, in which child care is often shared by grandparents, siblings, or other family members, it's considered quite normal for children to form strong attachments to adults other than their parents. And following this example doesn't mean that you are losing control, because researchers have shown that children start to understand something of the complexity of inter-family relationships towards the end of the second year. A study in the Solomon Islands, for instance, which looked at children who were regularly cared for by their older brothers and sisters, demonstrated that even very young children could understand how the command structure changed with circumstances. For example, children as young as 18 months knew that when mother and father were not around, older brothers and sisters were in charge. But when they returned, the children refused to obey instructions from their older siblings.

Multiple bonds don't just have psychological importance, but practical advantages, too, because they provide additional security. If, for example, something should happen to the parents, it is very important for the child's well-being that another loving, sensitive adult member of the family is available – one who knows the daily routine and can take over as a substitute parent. Strong bonds with members of the extended family are especially important for the child of a single parent, because sometimes the child of a divorced or widowed parent becomes insecure and fearful about being left alone. Relationships with other caring adults – and children – in the extended family can help to alleviate this insecurity.

Below It's important that children learn to trust someone who might have to care for them in their parents' absence. And letting grandparents take charge of your baby not only gives them great pleasure, but allows you to have a well-earned rest.

Guardians of the family heritage

The relationships between grandparents and grandchildren are particularly special and important. Grandparents get great satisfaction from seeing a new generation of their family, and

grandchildren get to know about their heritage and traditions, and enjoy a special type of attention in return. There are advantages for you, too. A grandparent is usually the first person to turn to if you need someone to care for your child, and many new parents find that the shared experience of having and bringing up a child brings them closer to their own parents, from whom they can get valuable support and advice.

Sometimes, though, there is conflict – generally when grandparents have different ideas about parenting from you. Approaches to the subject have changed many times over the last few generations, and although minor variations, rules and regulations may be good for children, because they teach them to be adaptable and appreciate that not all people are the same, an approach that is very

Above *Time spent with a grandparent allows a child to form a very special bond. He or she will not only learn to interact with older people, but be entertained and educated by their views and stories.*

Right *In Mediterranean countries, where the extended family is still a major force in society, bonds form and grow across the generations.*

different from the usual one can be unsettling. A child whose parents do not insist that everything is eaten at mealtimes, for example, will become confused and upset if grandparents insist that the plate is clean. The solution is to discuss your ideas of parenting with grandparents, and ask them tactfully, but clearly, to make sure that there is consistency.

Unconditional and permanent

Children learn a lot about family relationships from seeing the rapport you have with your

parents and relations. If you enjoy secure, loving relationships with close kin your child will feel more secure about his or her place in the family – and it is important for a toddler, who is developing a sense of "self" to have a sense of belonging to a large group, and discover his or her place in that group.

But one of the most important benefits your child will receive from forming bonds with its extended family is an appreciation of the permanence of a family's unconditional love. Your child will see that its grandparents still love and care for you, even though you are grown-up and a parent. This will show that love and care – as well as responsibilities – are there for life, and are not just switched on and off at a whim.

Making Time for Fathers

It's all too easy for a mother to devote herself to her new baby to the exclusion of everything else – and that can include her partner. Partly this is an expression of the fiercely protective love that most new mothers feel (*see pp.14-15*); but partly, too, it is a survival from the days when men went out to work and it was exclusively women who cared for babies – something that persisted into the lifetime of most of our grandparents.

Today, things are different. It's generally accepted that men have a role to play in baby care – in theory, that is, but not necessarily in practice. Even if they want to help, men often seem to have a lack of confidence with babies, feeling that mothers instinctively know best and that they will be clumsy and inadequate by comparison, and make a mistake. And some mothers, too, worry about their partner's parenting skills and assume that they are the only ones who can cope. That's a pity, because it's important for bonding that fathers play a part in child care – not just so that the mother can have some rest, but because fathers bring something special and different to their relationships with their children: a deeper voice; a sense of extra protection; and an aptitude for rough and tumble.

Below *Fathers should be included in child-care as much as possible. Bottle-feeding, for example, is a simple and pleasurable way of promoting paternal attachment while satisfying one of a small baby's most basic needs.*

Jealousy

Sometimes fathers become jealous of the relationship between their partner and their child – and often it's for a good reason. A baby is the product of its parents' relationship, and should enrich it – the birth should never signify the end of the original relationship but its progression. Yet it's easy for fathers to feel left out, especially when mother and baby are the centre of attention, and there can be a feeling that they have been demoted. Many grandmothers (though not, I must say, mine) seem particularly prone to doing this, by bustling around and snatching the baby away from its father at the first sign of crying. The result can be that the father becomes resentful at the way he is being excluded, both from his partner's life and from his involvement with the new baby.

The answer is for both parents to make a deliberate effort to ensure that the father is involved as much as possible with the baby's care: feeding; changing; bathtime; bedtime stories; pram-pushing; and so on. Many fathers are less than adept with a baby at first, especially when they are only children – but the only way they learn what to do and develop confidence is to practice. But, if you're a mother, resist the temptation to rush over and grab your baby if it starts to cry.

Left New babies can seem to take over your lives and disrupt the pattern of your relationship. It's vital that you make a deliberate effort to plan time alone with your partner – for the baby's sake, as well as for yours.

A loving relationship

As I've said, a child bonds best when it lives in a harmonious household in which there is a loving relationship between its mother and its father. And that means that you must also pay attention to the sexual relationship between you and your partner, as well as coping with the day-to-day business of child-care.

It's fairly common for new mothers to lose interest in sex for a while after a birth – in Britain, doctors normally advise women to wait for a check up at six weeks after the birth, anyway. However, some mothers find that they cannot revive their sex drive – sometimes because they're exhausted (and a man who never helps can seem less than attractive); sometimes for hormonal reasons. If you suspect the latter, consult your doctor. But if you or your partner are just too tired to make love, it's important that you make time for each other and have a break from your baby.

Plan an evening together, hire a baby-sitter *(see pp.88-91)* and enjoy yourself – or retire to your bedroom during an afternoon when your baby is asleep. If you're the father, remember that your partner will probably need reassurance about her attractiveness; if you're the mother remember that he might well be feeling a little insecure. However you play it, make sure that you allow time for your relationship to be reinforced and to grow.

Single Parents

I have to declare an interest: I'm a single parent. I was divorced seven years ago, and I have five children. But the scientific evidence is clear: as far as baby bonding is concerned, all children would have two parents ideally, and they would live together in harmony and affection.

First, babies need to form a bond with two people of the opposite sex – studies even show that babies need to hear, regularly, both a high-pitched, female voice and a lower, male voice. Second, research shows that babies need the security of being part of a loving relationship between two adults; a partnership that provides an example for relationships later on in life, and gives a child an adult man and woman to act as role models.

However, it has been believed for many years that it is bad for a baby to be a part of a discordant, unhappy family unit – though new research has cast a different light on this idea (see pp.132-135). Babies are much more sensitive than you might think to tension and dissension – in fact discord can often contribute to illness and anti-social behaviour (doctors talk of the "dysfunctional family"). On the other hand, there is considerable evidence that delinquent, socially disruptive children come from single-parent households more often than not. In the case of single mothers, it is not just the lack of a father-figure that causes problems, but other factors: sole responsibility for care;

Above *Try to involve your child if you work at home – even though it can be irritating and difficult at times. Small children love computers: a word processor is ideal for helping with letters and learning to read.*

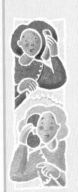

Support systems

Sometimes the demands of coping single-handed, together with the need to earn a living, can overwhelm a single parent. But don't despair: help is available.

Ring your relatives and friends (swallow your pride, and call your absent partner, too, if you have one) and ask them to come and babysit for a few hours, so that you can get out and enjoy some free time.

Next, look in the 'phone book and contact all the government and local agencies you can. Tell them about your problems and ask for the names of local single-parent groups and support systems. You'll find that there are single parents with the same problems as you in most towns, who can give help, advice and practical assistance.

youth; poverty (the most significant factor); little time for communication and
stimulation. But on balance, I still believe that separation and divorce can be the best
thing for your baby if the relationship cannot be saved.

Confronting the problems
It isn't the end of the world as far as your baby's bonding is concerned if you are a single
parent, so long as you confront the three main problems: isolation, exhaustion and the
lack of a role model of the opposite sex. The potential for isolation varies, depending on
the role of the extended family *(see pp.76-77)* in individual societies. If you can, enlist the
help of relatives; if not, ask friends; use the facilities provided by government and local
associations; and, if you can afford it, hire a nanny – they're not all frightening women
with starched aprons.

Doing this will also make it much easier for you to work and reduce the feeling of
helplessness and exhaustion that can overwhelm a single parent. It can also give you that
vital time for play. At the least, carry the baby round as you do the housework, and try to
involve him or her when you work.

The other main problem is more tricky. If you are separated, your absent partner can
provide the role model. But the difficulty comes with your own relationships. A new
partner can provide a role model over the long term. But, inconvenient though it may be,
short affairs are very unsettling – curiously, much more so for boys than for girls. The
result can be that your child demonstrates an excessive need for approval and praise,
because what you are doing can make it look as if all bonds are
impermanent and insecure.

The same applies to the absent partner. But, if you are
one of these, you're in a good position to form a strong
mutual attachment – though this might seem hard to
believe at first. Without the chores of care, you can
concentrate on talking, playing and going out – but it's
vital you see the child regularly.

It is important, too, not to raise the
emotional temperature and become too
intense. Remember that your feelings are
your own, not your baby's. So respect
the difference and don't demand
undue affection. High emotion,
frequent demands and clinging adults
make toddlers and children anxious.
To bond successfully you must be a
safe haven and a role model, giving
comfort, reassurance and stimulation.

Below An absent parent
(and usually that's the
father) is in a wonderful
position to form a good,
positive bond with his baby
– with no day-to-day routine
of caring and household
chores there's no obstacle to
play, communication and
cuddles.

Making Time for Yourself

In my experience, men find it easy to make time for themselves – they consider it their right to have a quick drink after work, play a game of squash or watch a football game. So these two pages are unashamedly written for mothers, who somehow feel that they have to ask, as if for a personal favour, when they want time off from childcare, and feel guilty when they enjoy themselves away from the family.

Working mothers are particularly prone to such guilt feelings – perhaps because they think that since they leave their families in order to earn money (which, by the way, very likely pays for basic necessities) they ought to spend every free moment with their children. And full-time mothers sometimes regard motherhood as their job, and feel they can never ask their partners to help just so that they can go out and amuse themselves. But all of us who work have holidays – so why shouldn't mothers have a break, too? Some people think that looking after children isn't real work, but if you've been stuck with young children for any length of time you'll know how exhausting and stressful it can be. As a mother you need time out to relax and just be yourself.

Below *However much you love being with your baby, it is vital that you set aside time for yourself. Read, visit friends, go to the gym – whatever appeals the most, but make sure you indulge yourself for a change.*

Martyrs to motherhood

Whether you're working or at home with your children, it's important that you don't make yourself a martyr to motherhood – no one will thank you in the long run. We all need to recharge our batteries, relax, socialize and amuse ourselves, not only for our own state of mind but also for the sake of all those with whom we come into contact. And however much you love your children, you will sometimes feel frustrated, tied down, fed up and bored. If you have no let up from these feelings, your relationship with your entire family will be affected.

A constant theme of this book has been that you must respond to your children's cues, but the converse is also true: your child must learn (or, rather, you must teach your child) to be responsive to your needs as well. Children who believe you are always at their beck and call, and are not used to sometimes having to wait for their demands to be met, will develop unrealistic expectations about relationships with others – and may well have problems with their playmates. Children don't want, and certainly don't need, "smother" love. If they feel that you live through them, and for them alone they will feel overwhelmed by this pressure and attached to you by guilt rather than

Left Ask your toddler to help you with the daily chores. Not only does this make a child feel useful and important, but he or she will soon realize that you can't devote 100 per cent of your time to childcare.

love. You need to do your own thing so that your family appreciates that you are an individual, who has her own special interests. Spending time away from your children will also help them to understand and appreciate independence. Because you are a role model, your children will learn from you, so if they learn to appreciate that you need time to yourself they will feel they can and should take time to care for themselves.

Time off from your children doesn't necessarily mean you have to leave the house. I had one rule that helped a lot: all my children, whatever their ages, either slept or played in their bedrooms for an hour after lunch – or their feed when they were babies. During that precious hour I ignored all the household chores and read, that being my passion, and at the end of the hour I felt I could tackle the rest of the day and night with zest and humour. The children accepted this as part of their routine and rarely interrupted me.

A burden shared ...

Although you may feel your child is ultimately your responsibility, it is important that your partner takes charge sometimes (*see pp.78-79*). He should enjoy looking after his child, but if he won't help, you'll have to force the issue. Don't feel guilty about this – both partner and child will benefit from a close, caring relationship. He must learn to cope with the essential day-to-day chores that go with looking after a child at home, just as you did.

Even if he always volunteers to help with childcare, a partner who has been at work all day and plays with his child for a short time in the evening may not understand your need for different surroundings. He enjoys being with the child, feels no desire to be away from the home and may well resent you organizing an evening out. You will have to explain that you sometimes need to pamper and enjoy yourself; that you want to spend time alone with him, have fun – and, eventually, sleep.

The Magic of Language

Throughout their first year, babies prepare for speech. Sucking, crying, mouthing toys, cooing and babbling all help to co-ordinate the tongue, lips and vocal cords. But although a baby's first recognizable words are an important milestone for parents, and are eagerly anticipated because they prove that the baby knows and understands them, in fact babies communicate long before they actually start to use words.

Tuning in to baby talk

Infants are predisposed to tune in to the sights and sounds of other people *(see pp.48-51)*, and part of what this teaches babies is the two-way nature of communication. A baby is able to determine whether or not an adult is trying communicate as early as the third month, so it's vital that you talk to your baby as much as possible. It doesn't matter what you say – the important thing is that your voice is heard frequently.

Initially, a baby's only form of communication with you is crying – the only way that needs can be expressed. Responding quickly to a baby's cries not only establishes trust,

Right Babies learn about communication by watching, listening and imitating. Brightly coloured moving images on a children's television programme provide an opportunity for your baby to listen to other voices and become aware of unusual sounds and shapes.

which helps form bonds, but also lets the baby know that communication is effective – which is why it's so important not to leave an infant crying for too long. But within a few months, babies start to learn about speech by imitation: at six weeks, babies often open and close their mouths, as if trying to respond to what you're saying; and by eight months, most babies have learned to read and react to their parents' expressions and tones of speech.

Most parents help their babies' language development without realizing that they are doing so. Studies have shown, for example, that mothers automatically raise the pitch of their voices and slow their speech when speaking to their infants, because babies hear high-pitched noises better than low ones. Mothers also tend to speak to their babies as if they were going to reply and leave pauses for answers when asking questions. This encourages responses and shows the baby that the mother is interested in what he or she has to say. Mothers also imitate the sounds their babies make, which shows the baby that language is important, and reinforces his or her attempts to communicate.

Above Pointing out pictures and making up stories about them shows your baby that you want to communicate and encourages language development as he or she listens to the changing tones of your voice.

Communication breakdown

If parent and baby fail to communicate, it becomes difficult to form a proper attachment. Mothers who are having trouble bonding with their infants often say: "I just can't understand him", or "I don't know what she needs". Often, the problem is that they are paying too much attention to what well-meaning friends, relatives and doctors are saying about the baby's requirements and are losing sight of what their baby is trying to tell them – and it's sometimes difficult to work this out, even if you're an excellent reader of cues. But when your baby starts to talk, the attachment between you will be all the more special, because he or she can now tell you about specific problems; personality can also be expressed, so that you will come to know your child on a far deeper level.

First words

A baby's first intelligible words will come around the time of the first birthday. At this age, children use simple one- or two-word phrases as sentences. For example, "Daddy" might mean "Come here, daddy", while "Daddy?" might mean "Where is daddy?". If you pay attention to your child's gestures, expressions, and inflection, you will probably be able to understand exactly what he or she is trying to say, much to the amazement of strangers who won't know your child as well as you do. You can encourage your child's language development by interpreting the meaning of the words used and adding to them. For example, if your child sees you letting the dog out and says "Dog", you can respond by saying "Yes, the dog is going outside". This lets your child know that you're listening, and that the attempts to communicate have been successful. Exchanges such as this are, of course, very important if your child is trying to express a need or desire, such as hunger, fear or pain. If the attempts to speak are interpreted accurately and responded to quickly, your child will gain confidence, and will attempt to speak more often.

The Israeli Experiment

An Israeli *kibbutz* is a collective farm or industrial settlement, in which work and planning are shared by the community, and, except for a few personal possessions, all property is communal. The first *kibbutzim* were established by the pioneers who founded the modern state of Israel in the 1940s, and one of their aims was to ensure that life for women was very different from that which they had experienced in the ghettoes of Europe, where they had devoted their lives to their husbands and children. As a result, they developed a highly organized system of childcare – and one that met the need to use all available labour as efficiently as possible in order to survive.

Right Kibbutz children spend most of the day with their metapel but this does not seem to affect the parent-child bond.

In the early days of the *kibbutzim*, childcare devolved on to trained carers called "metapels", who looked after the children of the community so that mother were free to work alongside their husbands. Children lived away from their parents in special children's houses, but saw their mothers and fathers each day. Each of the metapels, who deliberately distanced themselves from their charges, looked after several children. Children moved through different houses as they grew older and had several different carers during their childhood, so learning to interact with different adults from an early age.

Metapels still look after children today, although now more care is provided by the parents. The system encourages independence and the children are soon taught not only the importance of collective activity but also of their own contribution to their community. Members of the *kibbutzim* share the belief of those in non-industrialized societies that children belong to everyone.

In fact, although family members spend much of their time apart, the *kibbutz* community is family-oriented, and the importance of parent-child bonding is recognized. Children who live on a *kibbutz* are usually breastfed, which allows time for close interaction between mothers and their babies, and some *kibbutzim* use an original system to alert mothers that they are needed: a metapel raises a flag individual to a mother when the baby needs a feed, in order to call her in from the fields. Although the babies are generally weaned by the age of six months, so that the community does not lose valuable full-time labour for too long, a strong mother-child bond will have formed during this time.

Today, about five per cent of the total population of Israel lives on *kibbutzim*, and although they are becoming less strictly communal the sense of shared responsibility is still very strong. The approach to childcare, though, has softened: now, children spend two hours a day with their parents and most of the day with them on the Sabbath. In some *kibbutzim*, children are allowed to sleep in their parents' living quarters. Communal dining rooms, which gave adults the chance to relax and interact with others, are used less often – instead, parents take plates of food back to their own rooms and eat with their children.

Above Kibbutz children learn to be happy and independent away from their parents and interact constantly with others of their age group.

Intensity and quality

The institutionalized child-care developed in the *kibbutz* has given experts new insights into parent-child relations. Although it was once believed that parent-child bonding could only take place under specific conditions, it is now thought that a bond that grows out of a parent's love for a child is strong enough to survive daily separation.

In his 1951 report to the World Health Organization, Dr John Bowlby, an eminent English psychologist, claimed that infants who aren't cared for sufficiently often by their mothers subsequently suffer psychological problems. He had already suggested, in the late 1940s, that institutionalized children were unable to form attachments on account of the number of carers with whom they came into contact. In 1969, however, in a report with a very different emphasis, Bowlby said that children raised on a *kibbutz* were more attached to their mothers than to their metapels – even though they didn't live with their parents. There is no evidence that children raised under the *kibbutz* system suffer any long-term emotional or psychological damage, or that they are in any way abnormal in their development.

Experts now believe that it is the intensity and quality, rather than the amount, of the time parents spend with their children that is important, as well as the quality of the institutional care they receive. Parents living on a *kibbutz* don't have to worry about working, cleaning the house, or preparing meals. They are able to give their children their full attention and devotion during the allotted time they have together, and this allows strong bonds to develop.

Sharing Responsibility

It is very important for a child to understand that while mummy and daddy are best other adults can be trusted, and even loved, and that it's alright to feel happy about spending time with them. There are several reasons: first, such a child tends to be much more sociable and confident than one who has only ever spent time with his or her parents, who often finds it difficult to relate to, let alone bond with, other people. Second, you should think about what would happen in the event of illness or accident, when there would be no alternative but to leave your child with someone else. In this event, the adverse effects of any separation would be greatly lessened if the person who takes over knows the child, his or her likes and dislikes, routines and the way your home is organized. And, third, you need to spend some time alone with your partner (see pp.78-79;82-83), both in order to relax and to retain a sense of your own identity.

The answer is to find a part-time carer (my apologies for this horrid word, but I can think of no other) whom you feel is happy with your baby when you are away and *vice versa*. This will not be a problem for your baby – infants are quite capable of forming numerous attachments, but their nature and strength depend on the personality of the adults and their emotional involvement, sensitivity and responsiveness. And how long you spend away from your baby depends very much on common sense – most mothers will know instinctively if they are not spending enough time with their baby, especially if he or she starts to become anxious having previously been confident and outgoing.

Above Before employing anyone to look after your baby, you must ensure that you share certain opinions on childcare and know that you have implicit trust in the person you choose.

Opposite Young babies soon become used to a regular carer and should be happy to be left with them – they will only become upset if there are frequent changes of nanny and their routine is broken.

Time for introductions

Unless it's completely unavoidable, don't leave your child with another carer for the first time during the anxious, clingy, "mummy" stage, at around nine or ten months, when he or she is in the process of forming a strong bond with you. During this stage, which only lasts a short time, infants are usually suspicious of other people, and may kick up a fuss when you leave. And the fuss created, as well as the distress behind it, is likely to be much greater if the child has been used to the full-time attention of its mother. So it's much kinder to introduce another carer before six months, even if you're at home the whole time. At this age, before an infant is fully able to appreciate you as the mother or father, and before you have fully bonded with each other, he or she will accept being left with a babysitter without too many problems. And if the same person cares for the baby on a regular basis, the two will become familiar with each other. Once the alternative carer becomes part of the routine of day-to-day living, the infant will accept these temporary

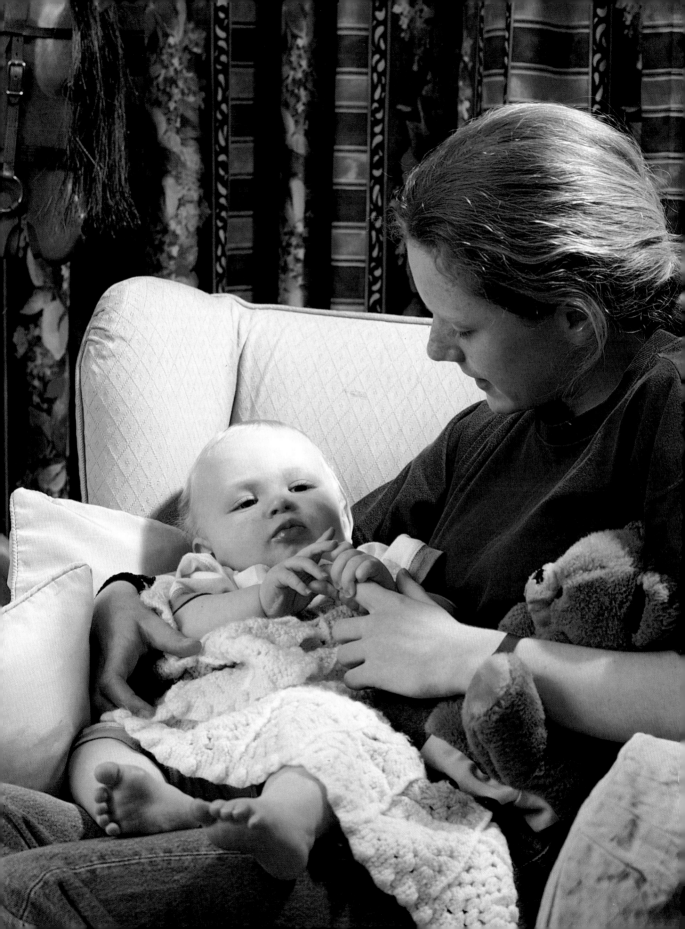

separations, knowing that you will return. So always tell a child beforehand that you are going out, and say when and for how long – even if you're not quite sure that your infant understands what you are saying and you hope that he or she will sleep through your absence anyway. Whatever happens, don't abandon the idea of going out because your child is making a fuss at your leaving. Be sympathetic and reassuring, but firm, and point out that you need some time away to be by yourself.

Below Many women return to work after they have had a baby – some from choice, many from necessity. Try not to feel guilty about leaving your baby: provided he or she feels secure with the carer, the mother-child bond will not suffer.

Essential qualities

You can pick and choose from a number of different kinds of carer, depending on your budget and availability. Among the possibilities are a local babysitter, a relative, an *au pair* or a nanny – all of whom will probably be able to look after your child in your own home. Otherwise, you could consider taking your child to a local childminder (a registered one) or to a creche – both partners should talk over the options and decide what is best.

Whatever route you take, some qualities are essential in the carer you choose. She, or sometimes he – men are not precluded from this role – needs to be reliable, warm, cheerful, adaptable and have common sense and initiative. You also need to get on well

with each other – although you don't have to be bosom buddies there does need to be a friendly atmosphere between you, as well as trust and mutual respect.

It's important, too, to check whether you both hold similar views on the practical aspects of child care. If you disagree on fundamentals, such as discipline, manners, whether or not to feed on demand and routine, the arrangement is unlikely to be successful, because you'll spend your time worrying whether the carer is doing what she or he has been told. And a trouble-free relationship is not just important for your own peace of mind, but vital for your child, too, because he or she will sense any tension or distance between you and will either become anxious or, when older, use any unease to play one of you off against the other. What really matters is that your carer has love and warmth to offer your child. Allow for some mistakes, though – after all, nobody's perfect. Carers, have their off days, just like mothers, fathers and children, so try to be sympathetic if they are grumpy occasionally.

The temperament, character and age of your child is also an important consideration. If your child is easy-going there should be few problems, but make sure that the carer provides adequate stimulation; if your child is highly active and demanding, someone with patience and energy is needed – fit the carer to the child. It's also worth remembering that young children, especially in their second year, develop their language skills rapidly, so it's not the ideal time to employ someone who speaks little of your language.

Mothers at work

Today it's quite usual for women to work after they've had children – though it was most unusual in my mother's day. Like men, many women want careers of their own and are just as committed to their jobs as their male colleagues. But when they become mothers, some such women are torn by conflicting desires and by guilt. And this is silly: there's no reason why they should feel guilty about going back to work after having a baby, if this is what they want. For many women, of course, there is simply no choice – the mother's income is needed to provide essentials and pay the family bills, and it's usually vital if a family is to have any chance of maintaining the standard of living enjoyed before having children. Other women believe that they need to work in order to feel happy and fulfilled – and it's surely better for a child to have a fulfilled and happy mother for part of the day than a full-time mother who is always miserable.

The evidence supports these beliefs: British researchers Anthea Holme and Simon Yudkin showed in a 1963 survey of children of working mothers that children suffered no ill effects if they were separated from their mothers for part of the day. In fact, many were more independent, self-reliant and less anxious than children who were looked after full time by their mothers. But there was one *caveat*: they also found that mothers with a full-time, demanding career were often too exhausted to cope sensitively with their children at the end of the day when they returned home from work.

A predictable world

If you're working, certain things need to be thought through and attention paid to them – for the sake of your child's well-being. Try to avoid passing on any feelings of guilt or anxiety – it's tempting to assuage such feelings by smothering rather than mothering your child when you are together. And sometimes you have to forget the concept of "quality time" – of coming home and attending to your child for a certain time each day. By all means set aside time to play, but bear in mind that he or she may not want to concentrate on you at that moment. Your child may be happy doing something, or playing with someone else, or simply tired or tetchy. If this is the case, make sure that he or she knows you are available, but don't push it. If a child is not feeling receptive or wanting your attention, no amount of pushing will alter the situation.

What a child needs from working parents is stability and consistency of care – in short, a predictable world in which to grow up. A child needs to know its carer, and to know when the carer is going to look after him or her – also where the caring is going to take place. Many studies have shown that babies and children who have had multiple and ever-changing carers fail to form close bonds. Instead, they are inclined to form indiscriminate, promiscuous attachments and often fail to reach their intellectual potential.

Above Parents may, understandably, feel anxious about leaving their child all day, but children at a creche learn to play and interact with others and may be more outward going than those cared for by their mothers full-time.

Teaching Your Child to Swim

Most new babies love kicking their arms and legs around in water, as you'll see at bathtime. And a baby who loves a bath will soon be ready to go swimming. Learning to feel comfortable in the water, and then to swim, has obvious practical benefits: first, all children should be able to swim, for their own safety; second, swimming is a wonderful form of exercise, which builds muscles, develops co-ordination and fitness, and aids physical development.

But teaching your child to swim is also an aid to bonding, because it is an activity that parents can share with their children – one that is stimulating, entertaining for all and an introduction to the outside world; it also provides an opportunity for your child to socialize and play with peers. And babies and toddlers usually feel relaxed and tired after being in the water – so you might get some peace and quiet once you return home.

Right Don't plough straight into the water on your first visit to a swimming pool. Sit on the steps or at the pool side and let your baby splash around for a while to get used to what's going on.

Left Don't use a float for the whole time: babies feel secure with someone holding them and enjoy splashing around on both their fronts and their backs.

The odd splash

If you have access to a heated swimming pool, in which the water is as warm as that of your baby's bath, you can start teaching him or her to swim as early as six weeks after the birth. Otherwise it's best to wait until the sixth month, because by this time a baby's temperature control has stabilized sufficiently to cope with the cold water of a normal swimming pool. You can use bathtime to prepare for the pool, though – get your baby accustomed to having a wet face and feeling the odd splash of water on the head, because these are unavoidable in a pool.

It's best to choose a swimming pool where there are mother and baby and mother and toddler classes – they can be found in most towns. Classes can be great fun and are especially useful if you're not very confident in the water; they can also be a good way of meeting other parents who have children of a similar age to yours. Generally such classes have the pool to themselves, or an area is cordoned off for them, so that you don't have to worry about other swimmers.

Above Get your baby used to being lifted up and dropped back into the water.

Swimming aids

It's a good idea to put your baby in a buoyancy aid to learn about going under water – I used to put arm bands on my babies, which they wore both in the bath and around the house before going swimming for the first time, in order to get used to them. When you buy buoyancy aids – you can usually obtain them at swimming pools where classes are held, but

Right Make sure that you buy a buoyancy aid that is appropriate for your child's age, and one that conforms to safety standards.

Above There's no need to teach your child proper strokes – a dog paddle will do. The most important thing at this stage is to instil a sense of confidence in the water.

check first – make sure that they are appropriate for the age of your child and that they adhere to the proper safety standards. It is best for your children to use safety buoyancy floats half the time they are in the pool to give them independence in the water, but do keep them free of support the rest of the time. This will prevent the children from using the aids as security blankets and at the same time they will gain confidence splashing around in the water by themselves.

Into the water

Your baby may seem a little anxious when you first get into the water, so take things gently. Above all, though don't give your child the impression that you're at all scared yourself, as your worries will quickly comunicate themselves to your child. Cuddle him or her close to you at first, then gradually increase the distance between you – though still holding on tightly – as your baby relaxes and gets used to the temperature of the water. Next, sink down into the water so that your faces are level; hold your baby away from you and then gently pull him or her back towards you and into your arms – first face-up, then face-down. Later on, try jumping up and down in the water while holding your baby, making waves and splashing around. Once your infant is relaxed and starts to enjoy the new experience you can be more adventurous. Start with your baby sitting on the side of the pool, keeping a good hold, then let him or her fall into your arms in the water.

SWIMMING TIPS

- Dress your child in clothes that are easy to take on and off and take a large towel to swaddle the baby for warmth.

- Take a ball or a waterproof toy with you so that you can play games in the water – your child will gain confidence by playing with a familiar object, and forget to be nervous.

- Choose a pool that has a special baby and toddler area – the water will be warmer and there'll be less splashing.

- Do not take a baby swimming for six weeks after a polio vaccination – the polio virus can persist in stools for this long.

- Remember to take spare nappies for afterwards, and make sure your baby's swimming costume fits tightly in case there's an accident. Don't worry too much about urine in the pool, because the chlorine in the water will neutralize it..

- Never let your child swim in the heat of the day in a hot climate, as small children burn very easily. Apply maximum-protection sunscreen 20 minutes before going outside, and reapply it after towelling your child dry. A sun-proof swimsuit is a good investment.

- Don't use sunscreen on babies under a year, because of the danger of chemical effects – only take such children swimming in doors or in the shade.

A sense of confidence

If you are teaching a toddler to swim, get him or her to jump into the water from the side of the pool, with you there to catch as the child hits the water. Show how to hold on to the rail at the side of the pool and kick with the legs, making as much of a splash as possible. Then teach your toddler to duck his or her head under the water.

The object of the exercise at this stage is to instill a sense of confidence in the water. All you need to do is show your child how to kick with the legs and to move the arms in the manner of a rudimentary breaststroke or dog paddle, so that he or she is mobile. There's no need to teach proper strokes – mobility, enjoyment and confidence are the only things needed, although it's certainly an advantage for a child to feel comfortable on both the front and the back.

A word of warning, though: a baby shouldn't stay in the water for longer than 20 minutes, because after this time body temperature begins to cool down and the baby starts to feel cold; half an hour is the maximum for a toddler; while children over the age of three can usually stay in the water for about three-quarters of an hour or a little longer. Remember that young children and babies don't usually complain about the cold – they just go quiet and listless – so keep an eagle eye on your child and take him or her out of the water as soon as you think it is necessary.

Below *Although swimming aids give confidence initially, if your child becomes reliant on them it will take longer for him or her to learn to swim unaided.*

V

TODDLERS

LOOKING AFTER A toddler is like trying to control a whirlwind. Once your child has learned to walk, the world seems like a vast playground designed purely for his or her amusement. Though it's right that your child now becomes more independent, the bonding process still plays a vital role, because your support is needed to help him or her explore this new and exciting world.

At this age, toddlers are gathering enormous amounts of information from numerous sources, such as a playgroup, reading and days out with the family, and now is the time when your child has to learn that problems sometimes arise. But a well-bonded child, who knows that there is an adult nearby to act as guide and comforter, will be secure when leaving his or her parents to walk through the school gates for the first time.

Reading and Television

Learning to read not only broadens your child's knowledge and promotes intellectual development but also provides opportunities for parents and children to spend time together. And a child brought up to love books will find them a source of pleasure, stimulation, solace and comfort for a lifetime.

Listening to a story helps to prepare for reading, and all children love the concentrated attention they receive when someone is reading to them – it needn't just be a bedtime treat: read to your child as often as you are able. Shops and libraries supply a wide range of books, so try them all and see which types appeal the most to your child. Some fairy stories may seem a little frightening, but they don't usually upset children. A story of a wicked step-mother or monster, for example, allows a child to feel scared, but not too scared, because he or she realizes it's not part of the real world.

If you're concerned that something specific is worrying your child, reading a story, or making one up, about the subject allows you to bring the problem out into the open. As the problem is related to the story, your child should feel less inhibited about discussing it, because it never has to pinpoint his or her anxieties directly. And books or a made-up story can also be a very useful tool for teaching social skills such as manners, sharing and the difference between right and wrong.

It's well worth starting to teach your child to read before formal schooling begins, but bear in mind that reading should always be fun. Forcing a child to read before he or she is ready and willing is rarely effective, and may put your child off books for life. If a child senses that reading is extremely important to you, he or she will either try hard to gain your approval, or will refuse to have anything to do with books at all. Learning to read should be something positive and pleasurable; it should not be a battleground.

Below Learning to read should be exciting, not an endurance test. Your toddler will enjoy looking and listening and also be happy that you are spending time with each other.

The electronic babysitter

Children today read far less than when I was young, and the place of books in many children's lives has been usurped by television. Nowadays, children spend so much time watching television that it acts like a babysitter. And it's not hard to see why – when a meal needs preparing, the floor washing or there's the ironing to be done, it's very tempting just to switch on the television and do whatever needs doing in peace. This may be convenient, but it doesn't help with bonding. Unfortunately, too, many programmes are unsuitable for young children: they contain scenes that are frightening and violent and that sometimes seem to encourage anti-social behaviour. There is much debate about whether such programmes encourage violence, but common sense would indicate that they do – certainly in the case of pre-school

Left Never feel your child is too old to enjoy being read to. And if children are encouraged to think that books are fun, they will develop a pastime that will stand them in good stead for a lifetime.

children, who have no clear idea of the difference between right and wrong and learn behaviour patterns through mimicry. Don't let your toddler watch such programmes.

But some television programmes can have a decidedly beneficial influence on a child's physical, social, personal and intellectual development. *Sesame Street*, for example, is informative and educational, and has been shown to improve toddlers' social skills and knowledge; other programmes promote pro-social skills such as altruism – doing something for someone with no expectation of a reward. Watch such programmes together, and talk about them just as you would about a book.

Get the balance right

So television for a toddler has its plus points and its minuses. The answer – as in most things – is to strike a balance. Too much television, and your child may become sedentary, fat and unfit: so make sure that there is a balance between television watching and outdoor physical activity; remember, too, that a child needs interactive play with other children and many other things besides a television screen – books, toys and relationships, for example – to develop his or her potential to the full. The wrong type of television programme, and your toddler may become violent, aggressive and anti-social: so choose television programmes carefully from the start and monitor them carefully, taking account of your child's age, character and temperament.

Above Tracing shapes or letters develops toddlers' communication skills while keeping them absorbed and entertained.

Exercise

A toddler seems to have boundless physical energy. Once the art of walking has been mastered, running will quickly follow – then your child will sprint down supermarket aisles, climb on to your sofa and into cupboards, never staying still. At this point you might find that gym classes – special parent and toddler gym classes are available in many towns – or more organized physical activities at home, help to divert your infant's energy into something safe and constructive.

But it's not only the practical considerations of saving your furniture and retaining your sanity that makes doing this worthwhile – there are a number of psychological, sociological and physical benefits, too. Your toddler will also be delighted, because most young children love physical play. A few need a little encouragement, but once they have become confident, all young children enjoy developing new skills, such as running, climbing, throwing and catching, and find them a constant source of entertainment.

New tricks
From the psychological point of view, the great thing about gym classes or organized play at home is that it's something new for your child that you can both do together. A toddler

Below Toddlers have inexhaustible supplies of energy, and organized gym classes are an ideal way to channel their exuberance away from wrecking your house. Physical play, especially with other children, is stimulating and immensely enjoyable.

Right New physical freedom found in play will encourage self-confidence – your child will delight in showing off his or her new skills to friends and family.

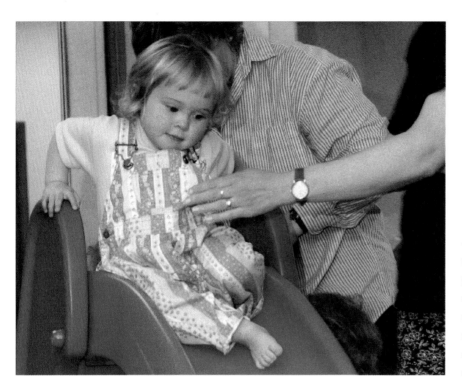

Left Gym classes are social events for both toddlers and parents, but, most importantly, toddlers can learn new physical skills while feeling secure in the knowledge that a parent or carer is close at hand.

who has become used to a daily routine will enjoy the chance to do something different, to go out and explore a new environment with a known and trusted carer. And as new movements are mastered, confidence, self-awareness and self-esteem will grow; great pride will be taken in showing off new tricks, such as cartwheels and somersaults, to other members of the family. Encouraging and helping your child to master new physical challenges will also give both of you a sense of achievement and pride in working together.

If no formal gym class is held near you, a local park or playground can provide a substitute. This need not be too highly organized – a playground with swings, slides and climbing frames and grass or sand to roll on are all that is necessary. But by setting aside a special time for physical play once or twice a week, you can show your child that you enjoy spending time together, and because there are no phones ringing or tasks to distract you, you can give your child undivided attention.

Gym classes can also be a good way of meeting other parents and new playmates for your child. Your toddler can learn how to interact with other children, as well as with other adults. For this reason, it is often useful for your toddler to take part in a gym class before starting in a playgroup or nursery school – he or she can get used to exploring new surroundings and meeting other children secure in the knowledge that mother or father is

Right Exercise is a vital part of a child's psychological as well as physical development. Classes ensure that both interaction with others and exercise itself are always great fun.

only a few steps away. Listening to the gym teacher and following instructions is also good practice for later on when your child starts at school.

A gym class or playground can be especially helpful to the parents of a new baby who find they have a jealous toddler, because, if you're such a parent, it gives an opportunity to have some special time on your own with your toddler. Not only will he or she have your undivided attention, but you can make it clear that even though babies might get more of your time, there are a lot of things they can't do, such as trampoline or catch a ball.

The physical benefits of organized exercise are also clear. Put simply, a child who has been encouraged by parents to be physically active feels secure and confident because his

Perpetual motion

Toddlers become more and more active once they start to walk, and their level of activity peaks around the end of the third year, when it approaches perpetual motion. When I was researching this book I came across a wonderful story of an international decathlete who tried to mimic all the movements of a three-year-old for a day, but gave up exhausted — my own experience makes this eminently understandable.

Tempting though it might be, parents shouldn't try to stifle a young child's urge to be physically active, although it is important to remember that everyone, including young children, needs calm and quiet times. Today many people believe that schoolchildren — and sometimes even toddlers — do not take enough regular exercise and are becoming couch potatoes, watching television and playing computer games. Too much of this is bad for children's psychological development, because they are not interacting with other human beings; and it is obviously detrimental to physical development, too. By encouraging young children to take regular exercise and playing physical games that they enjoy, such as catching balls in the garden, for example, playing hide-and-seek on a walk, or building sand-castles in a sand pit in the park — and making sure that this exercise becomes a routine part of their lives — you will be helping them to develop both physically and mentally.

Left Children who have been encouraged to be physically active are often at an advantage when they start school. They will have developed their co-ordination and a sense of spatial awareness, thus improving their self-confidence.

or her co-ordination is improved and he or she learns that things that might appear frightening are not necessarily so. Sports scientists talk of learning "spatial awareness", which means that a child develops an awareness of the three dimensions in which we live, and the necessary muscular and sensory co-ordination to relate actions to the space available and the objects present in that space.

Developing this ability gives a toddler a head start for when the time comes to go to school. Children who are active and perhaps a little more physically advanced than others of the same age are almost always popular with their peers. And hand-in-hand with physical ability goes confidence in dealings with others.

Exercise at home

Sometimes it's difficult to go to a park or gym class on a regular basis. An alternative is to find space at home where your children can climb, jump and roll without causing damage either to themselves or the room. If you want to play together at home, use a room full of mats and cushions – and choose one you don't mind being knocked about; if

you have enough space, designate one room as a playroom, or set aside part of the garden, and give your children free rein. Find an old chair for scrambling on, soft balls and rubber rings to throw, mats to roll on and for somersaults, climbing frames, hoops and so on.

One advantage of having a zone dedicated to children is that you will avoid many of the conflicts that might otherwise arise between your child's desire for physical play and your understandable wish to live in a house that has not been completely wrecked. When my children were young, I gave up any pretence at having a wonderful garden and there was one room in the house that always looked as though a hurricane had hit it, but I did manage to keep the rest reasonably tidy – and I kept my sanity.

Above Whether your child goes to gym or not, try to make sure he or she always has a chance to play outside, either in your garden or a public park.

A Family Day Out

TRAVEL TIPS

- Make sure your car is fitted with an approved baby's car seat or booster seat, according to age.

- If your child suffers from travel sickness, be prepared with paper bags, towels and a change of clothes – but keep them out of sight until they are needed. Don't make your child anxious by asking over and over again how he or she feels; instead, play games that involve looking out of the windows as a distraction. It sometimes helps if a car-sick child sits in front, as any swaying motion is generally felt less than when sitting in the back seat.

- If you're making a long journey by car, plan in advance for one or two rest stops along the way.

- Change your baby and give both baby and children a light meal just before you start your journey. Children are less likely to feel sick if they've had something to eat.

- Make sure there are no sharp objects around in the car that your children can play with and hurt themselves.

- Think about wearing your baby or toddler (see pp.60-65) when you reach your destination. In many places this may be easier than using a push-chair. And it certainly means less equipment to take with you.

Sometimes it's hard to spend sufficient time with your children, especially when they can be so easily distracted at home. And it's all too easy for a parent to lose a precious weekend doing household chores, reading the newspapers and watching the television. Taking young children on a trip, though, is an ideal way to ensure that the family is together, and is doing something together – with all the stimulation and interaction that this involves; free from interruptions, you can give your children the undivided attention they need and deserve. A day out provides a rare opportunity for a child to be together with both parents, which is especially valuable; and for a single parent, alone with a child at the weekend, just getting out of the house can be a tremendous relief – and that goes for the child, as well.

Right A family day out at the zoo provides a stimulating change from the routine of home-life and introduces babies and toddlers to exotic animals that appeal very strongly to young children.

Left *Time spent together as a family helps develop a sense of unity and security. In the bustle of day-to-day life, any shared experiences are very beneficial and will help to promote bonding within the family.*

A perfect day

A family trip needn't be elaborate or expensive, though it does require planning. Go to the park, visit the beach, or take a walk in the country – it doesn't cost anything – and for a child there's a wonderful sense of going on an expedition, especially if you plan the trip together, and use maps to show where you will be going and books to explain what you will see. A day away can be a perfect opportunity for your children to get to know your extended family, too, if you have relatives who live within a reasonable distance. You can also visit a zoo or a theme park to introduce your toddler to the exciting world outside your home – though as I know to my cost it can be expensive if you have a number of children.

A day out can also be useful when you have a new addition to the family. A special trip on your own with the older child can provide reassurance that he or she is far from forgotten amid the excitement of a new baby, especially if there is any feeling of insecurity about the change in the family structure. Later, regular outings with the older child and the baby will reinforce the idea of the family as a unit, and there is less likelihood that your new baby will be seen as an upstart or intruder. The older child will soon enjoy looking after the younger one and showing him or her around, and this will provide a sense of usefulness, importance and place.

Routine and Discipline

A number of elements must be in place if a child is to bond properly, and among the most important of them are routine and discipline. Routine gives a child consistency, and, therefore, security, while discipline enforces a framework of rules that defines acceptable and unacceptable behaviour and also provides constancy and certainty. Together, they give the confidence to explore the outside world from a solid base. That said, establishing routine and providing a disciplined framework for behaviour can often be difficult for parents and disturbing for children.

It's all a matter of approach and degree, though, and there are a number of pitfalls along the way. Most people – and I'm no exception – are far from consistent: we all have good days and bad days and ups and downs. Nevertheless, you must try. The only thing that kept me sane with five children, all predisposed to anarchy, was a strict routine of bathtimes, bedtimes and mealtimes.

Fixed points

With the arrival of a first baby it can seem impossible to get into a routine: babies don't read the books that tell mothers it's essential to do so and often refuse to co-operate; certainly mine didn't seem anxious to help. But as I found, once the baby settles down a little after the first few weeks it becomes easier to start a routine.

It's the parents who have to discipline themselves first and establish the routine. Once this has happened, though, many things become a lot easier – including the children, who

Right *Routines that are established at an early age, such as cleaning teeth, will be readily accepted as part of daily life. And not only do they provide security for the child but they make parenting a great deal easier.*

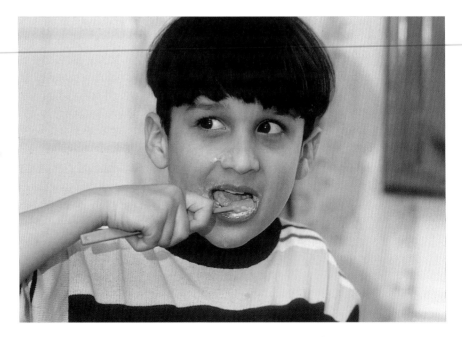

will happily accept something that happens regularly as part of their lives: be it visiting grandparents each Thursday; or lunch at 12.30 with a quiet time afterwards when mother reads the paper; and so on.

Discipline

When one hears the word "discipline", it conjures up a number of images: a Victorian father beating his son; or – to use a more contemporary example – a baby being left to cry alone because it's not time for a feed. These examples are extreme and rather horrible, but a sense of discipline is still important for a child: in order to function, every family and every society has to have rules that delineate what is acceptable behaviour and what is not.

For children to feel secure, both within the family and in the world outside it, they need to know and understand these rules. A child does not absorb an understanding of the difference between right and wrong and between different types of behaviour simply by observation, because what children see and hear is often inconsistent. No matter how much parents may try to be role models for their children, their assumptions and social skills are far too sophisticated for small children.

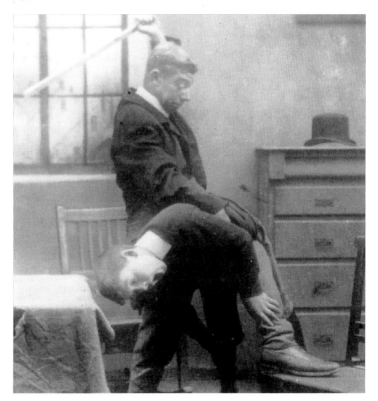

Above Nowadays images like this exist only in history books, thank goodness. Disciplining your child should be seen as a test of the bond between you – a bond that is built on sensitivity and trust.

So it is important that rules are laid down clearly. And when this has been done they must be obeyed and enforced consistently. Ensuring this happens is both an extension of, and dependent on, both the closeness of the bond between you and your children and your ability to recognize and react to their cues. Once children have formed a bond, it is possible to show them through example and parental approval (or temporary withdrawal of it) what behaviour is acceptable and what is unacceptable. It's important, though, that your disapproval is of the behaviour, not the child, and that the child understands this.

Methods of discipline (using the word in the sense of "enforcement" rather than a system of rules) must always be tailored to fit the age of the child. At all ages, though, love and a child's innate desire to please provide the best disciplinary opportunities. Punishments that cause fear may bring immediate results, but toddlers treated this way may well grow up to be subdued and lacking in confidence; at all times, punishment must be light, appropriate, sensitive and short-lived.

Right When you have to discipline your child, always make sure that "no" really means "no". Nothing will make your child lose respect for you faster than knowing that threats will not be carried out.

Above Even if a child is being deliberately naughty, try to be patient and avoid sending confusing signals. Ensure he or she knows that behaviour not personality is making you angry.

Namby pamby

My great-grandparents might well have thought this rather namby pamby, and said that I was spoiling children; some parents today would echo them. But it isn't possible to spoil children until they are old enough to appreciate individuals as separate people – at around six months, when they can form their first bond *(see pp.10-13)*. A child of six months who pulls your hair is merely practising a new skill, but a four-year-old who does the same is being deliberately naughty and seeking attention because of boredom, anxiety, jealousy or frustration.

Sometimes, of course, children behave badly, deliberately and without excuse – and it is natural for them to do so *(see pp.120-123)*. So what do you do? The first step is to explain clearly that what has been done is wrong and why you are unhappy. You must be careful not to get caught in a trap, though: a child always asks "why?", and sometimes the only response is "because I say so". That's not very satisfactory but it can be useful, because a sense of discipline is not only important to ensure a child becomes

A short, sharp smack?

Smacking is a controversial subject. Some people object to it on moral grounds; others believe that it infringes a child's rights. In some countries, such as Finland and Sweden, smacking is already against the law, and some campaigners in the European Union and America believe it should be made illegal.

Personally, I reject the argument about children's rights (at least in this regard), but concern about smacking is understandable: it's easy to believe that a quick slap can be the first step on the road to child abuse and battered babies. On the other hand, there are few mothers who haven't given a noisy, naughty toddler a slap on the legs when something seems the last straw at the end of a long, difficult day – and when the toddler then turns into a little angel wondered why they had never done so before.

I have smacked each of my children at some point in their lives, and each time I've felt terribly guilty and resolved never to do it again. But I can't see that it's done them any harm. They haven't taken my rare smack as a licence to hit others, or harboured resentment. Sometimes, because of its rarity and shock value, a slap on the legs seems to clear up smouldering resentments by releasing the tension for both child and adult, and so removes a cause of coldness and distance between the two. At the same time, the child is shown that the ultimate boundary of unacceptable behaviour has been crossed.

But there are some golden rules, and the first is that giving your child a smack should be done very rarely, very lightly and never on the face (I aimed for the legs), that it should be immediate to the problem and never done in cold blood in a formal, staged way. Second, there is never any justification at all for smacking a baby. Third, always cuddle children afterwards and tell them you love them, pointing out that you were cross with their behaviour not with them as individuals. Fourth, apologize if you were wrong – you will be on occasions – because doing so helps your child relate to you as an individual rather than as a symbol.

Finally, if you find that you are repeatedly smacking, and smacking too hard, stop completely and ask your doctor for help. If your emotions become uncontrollable, lock yourself away until you have calmed down. I used to put the children in their rooms and turn my radio up so that I couldn't hear their yells, read a book and return to the fray when calm.

socially acceptable, but for safety: it's no use explaining to children who are running across a road when a car is coming, but it is vital that they respond to "stop" immediately.

Love and careful explanations don't always work. Then you have to do something to reinforce your message. Smacking is discussed in the box above, but this is absolutely the last resort. The best thing is to apply cause and effect by withholding privileges. Children understand this, but the effect must follow the cause consistently. A useful punishment is to send children to their bedrooms, for a minute for each year of their age.

The better part of valour

My own theory is that the best way towards discipline is to avoid getting into a situation where confrontation is necessary, and to provide a distraction when it seems imminent. Avoidance techniques can also be developed by picking up cues, since most children are naughty when these are not being acted on. "Discretion is the better part of valour", you may say, and fair enough – but in this case, discretion is not cowardice, but practicality. If avoiding confrontation by manipulating a situation means that punishment is unnecessary this must be a good thing; it also makes it more significant when it is necessary.

Doctors and Dentists

Visits to the dentist or doctor can be very upsetting for children, and the presence of strangers, together with unfamiliar surroundings and uncomfortable procedures, often confuse and distress them. But there are a number of things you can do to prepare for such a visit, and help you to assume the protective and supportive role that your child needs and will have come to expect.

If your child is old enough to understand, talk about the visit as much as you can beforehand – it doesn't matter if he or she can't take in everything that you say. Read some of the excellent books that are available about visiting doctors and dentists with your child before the appointment, and rehearse what will happen by playing out the roles, using a favourite doll or teddy bear. Your child will be less anxious if he or she has some idea of what might happen beforehand. And make sure he or she is as comfortable as possible before the visit. Anyone who is tired, hungry or cold – and especially a child – is much more likely to become upset, even in the best of circumstances.

Right No-one looks forward to seeing the doctor or dentist, so it's vital that you keep your child as relaxed as possible before and during the visit. Bring a favourite toy, talk to your child and stay calm yourself.

Nothing to fear

Remember that young children are very good at picking up what you are feeling, so try to stay relaxed, even if you dread going to the dentist or doctor yourself. Be matter-of-fact and take a sensible, down-to-earth, nothing-to-fear approach, so that your child does not sense that whatever is about to happen is anything out of the ordinary, and keep this up throughout. If you think you won't be able to stay calm, ask your partner to go instead, or ask one of your own parents to go with you. After all, they've been through all this before.

Above all, though, never lie. If something is going to hurt, say so. If you lie, your child will lose trust in both you and the doctor or dentist. And, if a child feels pain that hasn't been expected, he or she will think something is wrong and probably squirm or try to pull away.

Try to maintain physical contact throughout the visit – whenever possible, hold your child. You will be the only familiar person, so make sure that you are constantly in sight. Bring along a favourite toy, such as your child's comforter, and a drink. And this is one time when a treat after the visit is a good idea.

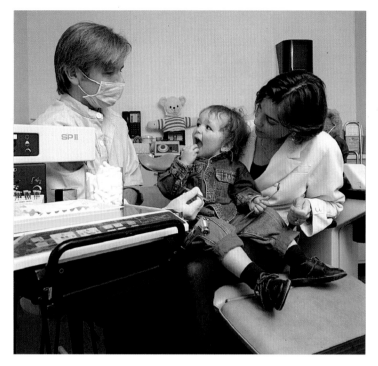

Above Stay as close as possible to your child during a visit to the dentist, to reduce anxiety and provide reassurance.

Children in hospital

Nowadays most hospitals make provision for parents to stay with a child during a hospital visit, so the bond between child and parents needn't be disrupted. This gives you the opportunity to help your child cope with unknown and possibly unpleasant experiences, and provides a fixed and familiar reference point.

Sometimes, of course, it just isn't possible to stay with your child. Research has shown that a short time in hospital, away from carers is unlikely to damage the attachments previously made if a child has bonded well. Occasionally, a child can revert to anxiety attachment *(see pp.10-13)* for a while afterwards. But if the separation from the carers lasts for a longer time – a matter of weeks rather than days – some children behave almost as if they have suffered a bereavement *(see pp.132-135)*: first, anger and crying are followed by apathy and dejection; then, seemingly brushing aside what may be viewed as a desertion, the child appears to forget about the carers and tries to forge new friendships. Once home from hospital and having being reunited with the carers, the child often ignores and repudiates them for a while, before a new, but rather insecure, attachment is formed. Trusting relationships have to be re-built before the child becomes securely attached to the carers once more. So don't expect to be welcomed with open arms when your child returns after a long stay in hospital: a great deal of patience is necessary, together with lots of love and extra attention, before things start to grow better and gradually get back to normal.

Giving your Child Roots

Below Religious ceremonies draw families together, giving children a perspective on their culture and their place in the framework.

A child's sense of security is based on love, self-esteem, self-awareness and, importantly, a sense of being rooted: a feeling of place or position in the world. In modern, industrial societies, families are growing smaller and usually consist of just the mother, father and children. While the bond between you and your child may be very strong, it's hard to give a child any sense of family culture or place in the family tree if the closest member of the extended family lives many miles away. Family traditions and culture may die out or be difficult to maintain if children move away from their parents to start their own households, instead of settling down nearby – as was once the case – so that the next generation was brought up surrounded by relatives. Often there are only very occasional and fleeting visits made by grandparents, and these are the only members of the extended family the child ever sees. So it often takes an effort to give a child a sense of belonging to a family unit that is larger than just two parents and, possibly, brothers and sisters.

Tales of long ago

One of the most effective ways of giving children knowledge about their roots and heritage is by telling them tales about their ancestors. Children of any age love stories, and are particularly fascinated if the heroes or heroines are related to them. You can make the stories even more interesting if

The stream of life

Western attitudes about the importance of cultural heritage and family tradition are very different to those held by members of traditional societies, where children are not taught about their culture or heritage in a formal, structured way but learn their religions and cultures from living in a close-knit community surrounded by grandparents, uncles, and cousins. In many parts of the world, mothers are not only responsible for childcare but also for giving children a sense of their social and cultural beliefs and customs. In India, for instance, where infant and child mortality rates are high, Hindus deal with the deaths of children in a religious context. Because of their belief in rebirth, each individual is seen as a part of a continuing stream of life. In this way, past and future generations are linked together with the present.

you have something to show them: my children love looking through old photograph albums, especially those of their parents when they were young in what must seem to them to be weird, old-fashioned clothes – to my frequent embarrassment. Old home movies, a family Bible or fading family letters can often be fun, too. You can use photographs or even drawings of relatives to make a family tree that will show your child how all the grandparents, aunts, uncles and cousins connect up as a family. Use an atlas to point out where the family came from originally, and where all the branches of the family and your relatives live today. If you have named a child after a particular relative, explain why, and tell your child what this person was like. Point out similarities in looks or mannerisms that are shared with past or present family members – but there's no need to go into detail about any of their stranger peccadilloes!

Religion and ritual

Religion creates a link between family members and is another part of the child's cultural heritage – even if it now plays less part in the daily life of many communities than it once did. Religious holidays are good times to remind children of this. On such occasions, special family traditions, such as eating certain foods, playing unusual games or visiting particular relatives, can make religion and its ritual seem more meaningful. It is useful to explain the religious significance of these holidays and the significance of the traditions that surround them. Knowing that mummy or daddy did the same things as a child, and that cousins are participating in the same ceremonies and celebrations, will give a sense of being connected to other family members in a very special way, even if the whole extended family cannot be together in the same place.

Special days of worship can provide golden opportunities to spend time together, as well as to remind your child of the family's religious roots. And religion – even at its most simplistic, in the early years – informs children of a family's cultural background and gives added security and sense of identity. This will be very valuable later on when your children go to school and encounter for the first time ideas and beliefs that are very different to, or sometimes opposed to, their own.

Below Many children love looking at old photographs and hearing how they are related to members of previous generations of their own family.

The Eastern Tradition

Traditionally, the Asian countries of China, Japan, and India have all stressed the importance of the family and family connections. A structured, extended family with many children remains the ideal. Families maintain links with numerous members of the extended family, which provides children with rich experiences and the chance to become attached to grandparents and many loving aunts, uncles and cousins. It's illuminating to look at how these traditional Eastern approaches to childcare work in practice today.

India and Pakistan

Living with a large, extended family has always been a part of traditional Indian and Pakistani cultures, and the importance of families and children is stressed throughout the whole subcontinent. Although women are generally considered morally and spiritually inferior to men, they are revered in the home. A mother has complete control over her children and household, and provides a relaxed, lenient, loving environment in the midst of a rigid, patriarchal society. The mother-son relationship is considered to be more intense than any other one in the family. Most girls leave home eventually, but sons bring their wives to live with the family, and stay with their parents for years to come.

Above *The extended family is a feature of Indian and Pakistani societies, and makes it easy for children to form multiple bonds.*

Babies are fed on demand and never left to cry on their own – they are breastfed for as long as two years, sleep with their mothers into early childhood, and are worn by their mothers or other members of the family during most of the day, and as a result multiple bonds form quickly and easily. Children aren't forced into early independence, or given very much formal instruction on how to behave in a socially acceptable way. Instead, young children learn by observing the flurry of activity of the extended household that surrounds them constantly, and there are always brothers and sisters, aunts, uncles, cousins, and grandparents around to ensure they are happy.

Japan

The elaborate, patriarchal network of extended family connections common throughout Japan's history was partially broken down after World War II, perhaps because defeat tended to discredit the country's authoritarian traditions. And with US occupation came new equal-rights laws, including one forbidding discrimination based on family status.

In spite of these changes, the extended family is still very important to the Japanese, and it includes dead as well as living relatives. Most modern Japanese homes have a family shrine – a corner devoted to the family's ancestors. A large part of a Japanese wedding ceremony is devoted to the couple kneeling before a shrine and announcing the union to their ancestors. Even now, a large proportion of marriages are still arranged, often by a grandparent or uncle, though today the arrangement usually only consists of introducing the couple – they are then allowed to make up their own minds about each other.

Children are at the centre of Japanese family life, and the relationship between parents and children is considered more important than that between husband and wife – which is perhaps why divorce rates are so low in Japan. The bond between mother and child is very special – it's a Japanese custom for hospitals to give a new mother a wooden box containing the umbilical cord of her new-born as a symbol of their special attachment. She expresses this by devoting herself completely to her children's care, and is responsible for their acquisition of social skills.

China

Children play a very important part in Chinese culture. They have always been appreciated – in fact, ante-natal clinics were established around 1,000 years ago to ensure that mothers-to-be felt at ease with their pregnancies, because their emotional state was thought affect the health of their babies. And in 1949, the ideal of a stable home life was reflected in a marriage law that made Chinese husbands and wives equally responsible for the care of their children; men are not permitted to divorce their wives while they are pregnant, or for a year after the birth of the child. But since 1981, when a law was enacted that limited the number of children to one in each family, children have not just been appreciated, but treasured – to the extent that children are often extremely spoiled.

A woman's relationship with her mother-in-law is still very important. In the past, the older woman would run the household and take charge of her son's wife. Today, young mothers often look to their mothers-in-law to do household chores and care for children while they go out to work. Sometimes both women work, in which case the grandfather takes charge of childcare. Parents rely on the children's grandparents to transport the children to and from nurseries, which are located within a working mother or father's place of business, and to take over during school holidays or when there is sickness in the family.

Traditionally, the father is regarded as the disciplinarian while the mother takes a more sympathetic role. Almost as part of a formal dance, she will often take the children's side in a dispute, and try to talk the father into giving lighter punishments.

Above Chinese children have always been treasured, but since the 1981 one-child law many of them have been downright spoiled – it's known as the "little emperor" syndrome.

A Problem Child?

Some children behave so badly that it's obvious they have a problem – and such children are known as "problem children". But that's a very loose and confusing term, and often doesn't mean what it seems to at first sight. The difficulty is to reconcile parents' expectations of behaviour with normal traits of childhood – and, of course, with the nature of the bonds that have developed within the family.

Many parents think they have a problem child when their child is behaving quite reasonably, because there's no consistency of expectation: one person might consider a child's habit of throwing food on the floor or constant thumb-sucking to be a problem; another might consider the same habit to be perfectly normal. In fact, such behaviour is quite normal for two-year-old – it would only become worrying if it continued in later childhood. At that time, the behaviour would be likely to be a sign of a lack of confidence and self-esteem, in which case the underlying problem would need to be addressed just as much as the symptom of behaviour itself. So whether you really have a problem or not depends on your knowledge of what type of behaviour is appropriate for your child's stage of development – if you're uncertain, ask your doctor, or consult one of the many excellent books available on child development.

Below Strong-willed children often vent their frustration with sullen defiance, before exploding into a temper tantrum. The answer is to avoid head-on confrontations whenever possible.

A pack of lies

Three traits in particular, which are common in childhood, are often seen as problems by parents. The first is lying: all young children lie (though "fib" would be more appropriate), and exaggerations, tall stories and fantasies are part and parcel of a young child's life. Notions of truth and falsehood and the distinctions between acceptable and non-acceptable behaviour don't start to develop until the second half of the second year and will even then be hazy, or over-ridden by other stronger emotions or desires, until the age of four or five.

It can cause problems if you over-react to fibs. Your child's understandable desire not to provoke anger or receive punishment will be much stronger than any desire to tell the truth, so fibs will be created to protect against retribution. And children know that their parents tell "white lies" – after all, we don't say "this is a pack of lies" before reading children a bedtime fairy story, and we pretend to believe in Father Christmas – but they have little

understanding of the difference between a white lie and what an adult would regard as outright dishonesty.

The second trait is stealing. Children who steal are more of a problem, though a toddler would normally think of taking something belonging to someone else as "borrowing". Toddlers want to have and keep anything that catches their attention and don't understand the concept of ownership – though it's something they have to come to terms with fairly quickly. Once you've found something that has been stolen, insist it is handed back to its owner. Explain why it has to be given back, but remember the explanation will be difficult to understand, and that if you make a mountain out of a molehill your child will hide the article from you next time. As a child's conscience develops, however, "borrowing" normally stops.

Above Bad behaviour that has become a habit needs loving firmness, extra reassurance and attention and sensitive handling.

Temper tantrums are the third childhood trait. Toddlers go through a stage of temper tantrums, and the stronger-willed the child, the more tantrums there are – and they can be very wearying. Try to avoid head-on collisions, if possible, but if your children have tantrums, don't expect them to pull themselves together: they can't *(see pp.106-109)*. Wait until the storm has passed and gently explain why whatever it is not possible. If you can think of one, suggest an alternative activity.

Question time

Once you've decided that some habitual behaviour is inappropriate for your child's age, that it's excessive and is not a childhood trait, you should deal with the problem lightly but firmly, bearing in mind that it is the behaviour, not the child, that is at fault. Then you must ask yourself some questions: are you too strict or too lax?; do you expect too much or demand too little?; are you giving enough personal attention, love and understanding?; do you know your child well enough?; have you given a sufficiently firm framework of rules?; are there too many rules?; are you and your partner consistent in enforcing these rules? And is the bond between you and your child sufficiently strong?

The answers may well be revealing – if so, you'll have to change your behaviour accordingly and discuss what the rules actually are with your partner. Sometimes, though – and it really is very rare – you may indeed decide that you have a problem child, in which case you should consult your doctor and seek professional advice.

Constructive Play

Play is very important for children, because it has educational as well as entertainment value – it's how they amuse themselves, but it's also how they learn. Children play in a variety of ways, depending mainly on the age, and the nature and style of play grows up along with them. During infancy, for example, babies play by watching and imitating what goes on around them, but when they are older they learn to interact with others and play with them. As your child develops you will probably see him or her playing alone with imaginary friends at first; next comes playing separately from other children, but watching and mimicking them; and in the final stage he or she will play confidently with other children and take part in organized games that have a definite purpose.

Below Don't be tempted to take over when playing games – you should be there to help and encourage but the ideas should come from your child.

Your role in your child's play changes as he or she grows older, too. During early infancy you will be the one to initiate a game, although you'll probably also find yourself reacting to your baby's cues, by, for example, talking about what your infant is looking at. Encourage your baby to take an active role in play by talking, singing, making faces, waving toys and through direct physical contact.

Babies are always intrigued by other children and will watch them with great interest, but until about the age of two few will play with other children. Toddlers are interested in one another, and will sometimes focus their attention on the same toy, but they aren't able to exchange ideas. At this age, they prefer to play with adults, who are usually more cooperative and predictable. So you will have a significant effect on the quality of your toddler's play.

A key to personality

Playing with your child, or watching your child play games, can help you to understand your child's personality. Your child can communicate many things to you and can show, for example, whether he or she is anxious, angry, frustrated, or content. Don't try to organize your child's play but respond to the cues and let yourself be led by the way he or she feels. If your child would rather bang lids together than play with the expensive, new stimulating toy you have just bought, so be it. Remember, too, that many things you might consider work are play to a child. So let your child try to help you with household chores – it will probably take you twice as long to get things done, but it's worth it for the extra time you can spend together and will help with bonding.

It's good to help your child explore new options with toys, but try not to interfere too much. In general, you should intervene only if your child appears to be getting frustrated or bored. If this is the case, suggest a destructive game to release tension and aggression – building something to be knocked down will often revive a child's interest, even though it may be rather annoying for adults who might prefer more constructive activities.

Above Toys that are noisy or that can be knocked around provide a harmless way to release aggression. They are cheaper to provide and often more fun to play with than expensive, "designer" toys.

In their second year, children begin to develop imaginary play, and from this age onwards, children engage in ever more complex games of make believe. Encourage these games, but make sure that you let your child's imagination work by itself. Young children have a very fuzzy concept of what is real and what is fantasy, so don't be surprised if you are introduced to an imaginary friend.

Challenging companions

If you have older children, encourage them to play with your baby to promote strong sibling attachment (see pp.14-15). Brothers or sisters who have formed attachments to each other are more sensitive to, and understanding of, each other's moods and feelings, so your toddler may be able to play with older siblings better than with other toddlers. And while a two-year-old is too young to initiate co-operative role-playing with a peer, he or she may enjoy taking part in a scenario created by a five- or six-year-old. In fact, some researchers have reported children as young as 18 months playing roles when they are being directed by an older sibling.

A toddler can also play in a more stimulating and advanced way with older children than when alone, and views older siblings as fun and as challenging companions. It's a good idea to let your children play with toys that aren't necessarily for the right age-group so long as they're safe: an 18-month-old can have as much fun with crayons and finger paints as a four-year-old. And a gift to one child of a toy that can easily be shared and which all can enjoy, encourages your children to become attached to one another.

Social Skills

Learning how to behave appropriately, both at home and in public, is an important part of your child's development. A securely bonded child will have confidence to form relationships outside the family, but it goes without saying that you cannot expect him or her to become a model of exemplary behaviour overnight. Manners and social skills are learnt progressively over a period of years, not weeks.

Nor is the learning process smooth, because children often go through a clingy stage – usually lasting for about six months at any time between nine months and two years – and refuse to leave their carer when in company; this happens whether or not the child has bonded securely. Be sympathetic and never force a child to socialize unless he or she wants to, as this will make for even more clinging. When the child feels sufficiently secure, he or she will leave you and play with others, but until then allow your infant to be a spectator.

Below Turn a lesson in manners into a game and your toddler will respond quickly and enjoy the time spent with you.

Appreciating feelings

At 18 months a child is still learning about him- or herself and has little understanding of the emotions of others. Even when they seem to understand how others feel, toddlers' reactions are notoriously unpredictable. A toddler may ignore one crying child, comfort another, and laugh at a third. Encourage proper behaviour, but don't expect your child to always display an adult reaction for a few more years. It is only in the second half of the second year that a child starts to appreciate that other people have feelings and realizes that there is appropriate and inappropriate behaviour. But good behaviour cannot, of course, be guaranteed even then – however much you may want your child to behave beautifully at formal gatherings, such as a family wedding. In fact your very desire to show off your child is likely to make you more anxious about any signs of inappropriate behaviour – and this anxiety makes it infuriatingly likely that your child will oblige by behaving as badly as possible.

Patience is a virtue

Just as children learn to communicate by imitating others close to them (*see pp.84-5*), they begin to acquire social skills by the same process. In one study, researchers observed that in the Solomon Islands babies as young as 20 months greeted unfamiliar visitors with the same courteous gestures as their parents. So it's a good idea to let your

Left Children can be demanding and selfish and are inclined to fight over possessions. Teaching your child to share is an important step in his or her development.

child get used to being with you when you're with other adults, in order that he or she learns that people are different and do not always react in the same way. Another difficult but important lesson to be learnt is not to interrupt while others are talking. Two mothers together are entirely capable of talking to each other and their toddlers simultaneously, while, for example, preparing a meal. But some adults don't have this ability and find the constant interruptions and noise annoying at the very least. If you respond quickly and appropriately to questions and demands when your child is

Above At gym classes and at school toddlers are encouraged to play with other children and overcome any shyness, since a parent or teacher is always on hand.

alone with you it can be hard for him or her to understand that there are times when it's necessary to wait. One minute, let alone five, is a long time for an infant – you can't expect a young child to wait for long and in this instance patience is not a virtue to be expected. Children are naturally inclined to want what they want when they want it. So in order that they don't try your patience too much, reply to their demands and questions with something other than just "wait". Give a reason why you can't respond, and say when you will be able to listen. Increase the time lag slowly as the child grows older.

Although your child will absorb some social skills by watching and imitating, certain things need to be taught – and the best way to do this is to make learning fun. If your child talks constantly, demands things and interrupts, try playing a game in which the child wins if silent for a given length of time after some music has been switched off. Keep a clock in sight, so that there's something to aim for, and give a reward – a hug, say – if he or she wins. Practice sharing and taking turns by means of a teddy bears' picnic: the child divides treats out among teddies set round in a circle. Play games in which the child loses occasionally, especially if with only children. And remember that other children wouldn't dream of letting someone else win altruistically, so you're not helping if you always let your child win. Losing gracefully is an important social skill, though no one likes to learn it – and some never do.

When your child is a little older, and doesn't mind being away from you for short periods, attendance at a playgroup can often help to develop social skills. Some children don't respond to advice given by parents, but learn quickly from other children. A child who is shunned by a group because of a refusal to share often decides playing alone is no fun, and quickly becomes more co-operative.

Above Babies learn many skills by imitation and it won't be long before they want to help you feed them, so be prepared for lots of mess.

Favourite toys

Supervised play with brothers and sisters or friends can help a child learn about sharing and taking turns, but don't expect your child to part a favourite toy. I used to hide my children's prized possessions when other children were around to avoid any problems. If there's a tussle over a toy, try not to intervene immediately but wait to see if the children sort it out for themselves. But if the situation seems to be heading towards blows, it's best to do something straight away – perhaps to offer another toy in exchange, or remove it altogether and suggest another game. A child who happily gives a toy to another either thinks the other child is stronger or is bored with it. But a child that always hands over toys immediately is either extremely placid – which is rare – or doesn't feel secure enough to stand up to other children, so may need more reassurance.

Table manners

Most children begin to feed themselves between the ages of nine and 18 months. In their second year, children learn to use a spoon well, and by about the age of three they start to use a fork. Children learn to feed themselves through imitation, although they sometimes require help and will definitely need lots of practice – so expect a lot of mess at first. It's useless to try to teach table manners before the age of two, because, a toddler won't be able to understand what is expected until then, or why. Playing with food is a part of learning how to eat, and harping on about table manners at too early an age will make eating an upsetting experience.

Once your child has learned how to use a knife and fork, start working on other skills, such as not reaching across the table to get something. There are a lot of rules for children to remember, so be patient. Try to be positive, and offer praise if your child says "please" and "thank you". Correct improper behaviour after the meal has finished with a gentle reminder – don't embarrass the child by scolding in front of company. Remember that children are eager to please.

Enjoying social relationships

Studies have shown that children who are securely attached to their parents display anti-social behaviour less frequently than those who have insecure attachments. Perhaps this is because an important part of having successful social relationships is the ability to interpret others' emotions and react to them appropriately – and this is something a securely attached child learns through the bonding process. Children who have strong bonds quickly learn to be sensitive to the cues of others, since their own cues are responded to with speed and sensitivity. If your child learns to love and trust you, he or she will be willing to love and trust others, and you can then help your child develop social skills by providing opportunities to meet other people. But a child who has an unresponsive, unpredictable and inconsistent carer has no reason to believe that others will be any different. The result is either an over-friendly or very solitary child, who is unlikely to consider the feelings of others.

Well-bonded children have enough security and confidence in themselves to enjoy social relationships and providing your child with these attributes is the most important thing you can do to help him or her develop social skills. Some children enjoy social activity more than others, so don't be concerned if your child seems to be a bit of a loner. All children take a few years before they use the correct social skills consistently. As long as your child isn't upsetting others with seriously anti-social behaviour, your silent reassurance and love will be much more beneficial in the long run than endless nagging.

Left A large family meal provides an excellent opportunity for younger children to see how their peers behave at table. But take care that you don't become so fussy about table manners that you discourage children from eating.

The First Day at a Playgroup

Children have an instinctive desire to socialize and learn, and a playgroup or nursery school can offer a wide range of stimulating learning experiences that are different from those at home. Playing with a group of other children builds up confidence and increases self-esteem and an independent attitude. It's best, though, not to start your toddler at a group immediately after a major upheaval in the family, such as the arrival of another baby or a move of house. Let your child get used to the new situation before he or she is presented with another new and stimulating experience.

The important thing is to ease your child gently into the new situation. A mother and toddler group, whether organized formally or a relaxed gathering with friends, is an excellent way of preparing your child for a playgroup or nursery school. He or she will soon become used to following instructions, accepting directions from other adults and playing with other children. This is especially useful if a child has had little social life and only one carer, since he or she may not have learnt how to adapt to different situations or to mix in with others, and may find it hard to accept being treated as one of a group and need help to socialize.

Below The first day at playgroup can be a traumatic experience, so comfort your child and try to stay until he or she has settled properly.

Making choices

Ask your friends for recommendations, then visit the playgroup and check carefully before making your choice. Is it friendly, relaxed and warm? Are the children allowed messy play, or is it unnaturally tidy? Are there enough adults for the number of children? Do you think your child will be happy there?

When you've made your choice, prepare your child for the first day. Visit the school together beforehand, so that both of you get to know the place and the carers. Point out activities that the child enjoys – as well as the ones that are new and might be interesting. Show where to hang coats, where the lavatories are and introduce the person who will be in charge. Above all, reassure your child that you'll only leave when he or she is happy for you to do so.

The first day alone

On the first day, however nervous or worried you are about your child, do not show it – a matter-of-fact and cheerful attitude is much the best. Even a secure and well-bonded child will feel anxious and be extra sensitive to your attitudes and mood. Staying for a short time, or even all

Left Learning music is a joy for most children, as they are encouraged to make as much noise as possible! Lessons at nursery school should be stimulating yet tremendous fun.

the time, for the first few days will make your child feel secure. Don't sneak out when his or her back is turned, as subsequently the child will never settle down to a task for fear that you will leave in the same way again. A child has little appreciation of time – though it often seems endless – and "I'll be back soon" has little meaning, so before saying goodbye and leaving, ask what the routine is for the end of the school session and say something positive, such as "I'll be back to take you home after the story". Be early – in fact, be one of the first parents to arrive – until your child has settled. Leave your telephone number with the person in charge, so that if your infant is upset you can be asked to come. But unless he or she is very upset indeed, it's best to stay with your child at school rather than take him or her back to your home.

Above Your child will enjoy the freedom to experiment with shapes and colours, and explore new subjects.

Once your child has settled he or she will enjoy the varied stimulation and company of other children as well as the fact that there is no time to get bored, while you can enjoy being by yourself for a change. Children who come from a home where painting and messy play is frowned upon will relish the freedom to experiment – if the playgroup is any good, while children from chaotic, unstructured homes will benefit from the order and routine provided. You will benefit, too, as you'll be a better companion when you have had a short time off from the constant activities and demands that most three- to four-year-olds make; a temporary absence from this age group can certainly make the heart grow fonder. And if you have another baby, a playgroup for the older child will give you and your baby some precious time alone together, as well as time to recharge your batteries.

Introducing a New Baby

If you decide to have another baby, the strength of the bond you have with your first child will prove to be very important. Older children who've developed some independence and a secure bond are usually less threatened by the arrival of a new baby than infants, who have yet to bond fully; children of three and over are much more likely to look forward to the birth of a baby; while children younger than this may be anxious about the prospect – according to the stage that bonding has reached.

In fact all children feel threatened by a new arrival to some degree, both during the pregnancy and after the birth and need constant reassurance that you still love them. (Curiously, one or two children – usually those over three – eagerly anticipate the arrival of a new brother or sister regardless of bonding, and are quite happy when the baby is brought home.) It's natural for a child to feel threatened by the birth of a brother or sister, even if the child is very independent and securely attached to both parents, because he or she will not like the idea of having to compete for affection. Although it's sometimes difficult, because it takes a lot of time and patience, it's essential to prove that you have just as much love for your first child as you do for your second. Provided you treat both children fairly, the older child will eventually come to appreciate the benefits of being a big brother or sister.

Below Encourage your toddler to become involved in your pregnancy. Letting him or her feel the baby kick and explaining what is going on inside you will make your toddler feel more secure.

Showing your love

After your new baby has been born it will inevitably be difficult to give your older child as much attention as before, and the difference in your behaviour is sure to be noticed. As a result of what they see as neglect, many children show symptoms of anxiety attachment after a new baby is brought home, with behaviour such as clinging and whining, increased thumb sucking, temper tantrums and sometimes even bed-wetting. These reactions to a new member of the family are quite normal, though it's a cause for concern if they don't disappear after a few months.

The most important thing for you to do is to demonstrate your love for your older child, while trying to meet the needs of both children – even though you won't always be successful. If your child openly expresses dislike for the baby, don't react with horror. It's much better that such powerful feelings are expressed outright. You mustn't give your child the idea that there are some things that might be felt but that can't be talked about.

Left It's vital that you give your toddler the opportunity to become involved in your new baby's routine. Imitating your actions will make your toddler feel important and more at home with your baby.

Preparing for the birth

You can help minimize problems later on by preparing your children for a new birth. But because young children have very little sense of time, don't tell your child you are pregnant as soon as you know it to be true. He or she is very likely to become bored with the idea within a month or two, and in any case won't understand that you have to wait for so long before the birth. A good time to tell your child is when he or she notices a change in your appearance – and this will almost certainly be much later than you expect. When the time comes, show your child pictures of babies in the womb, and look through children's books about babies together, to encourage an understanding of what is happening. If you have any friends with babies, ask if you can take your child to see them, so that he or she knows what to expect. And, if possible, bring your child with you to ante-natal appointments so that the doctor can show how the baby's heartbeat can be heard. You should also encourage your child to talk to the baby *(see pp.30-31)*, and feel the kicking inside your tummy. Communicating with the baby before the birth may help your child look forward to the new arrival, and lessen any jealousy when you bring the new-born baby home. Encourage your child to help you shop for anything needed for the new arrival, and let him or her choose a present to give to the baby after the birth.

Advance planning

A new baby certainly changes your life, but it changes the lives of any other children, too. It's likely, and understandable, that your child will resent any adjustments in routine that occur after the birth and blame them on the baby. The answer is to try to ease him or her into new routines before the birth, and plan all the practicalities in advance. Establish regular bath and bedtime routines with your children a few months before the birth. If you have the opportunity, start your child in a playgroup before the baby arrives, so that you'll be able to be with your baby without your child feeling jealous. Make arrangements well in advance with whoever is going to stay with your child while you are in hospital, and talk about this person to your child well before the baby is due. Think about sleeping arrangements: if you're going to move your first child into a bed, or a different room, do so a good few months before the birth, so there will be no feeling of the baby usurping the child's place.

Above Make your toddler feel special by explaining all the things that he or she can do that babies cannot – for example, walking, talking and playing games with you.

Happy birthday

When you go to hospital for the birth, try to make the time you are separated from your child as short as possible, because it's important that he or she doesn't feel abandoned. Phone calls from you and visits to the hospital to see you and the new baby are often helpful, but make sure that you're not feeding the baby when your child visits – it's best if your baby is quiet in the crib, rather than the centre of attention. After all, your child may well be more interested in seeing you than the new addition to the family. Take an interest in your children's activities, and make sure you say how much you've missed them.

A father's help during the first few weeks after the birth can be invaluable. Fathers can make sure that toddlers don't feel neglected, often with the result that the bond between a father and his first child grows stronger. Fathers, however, shouldn't take over as substitute mothers to the other children: if a mother only spends time with her baby, her relationship with her older children is likely to suffer.

A problem for girls

In one research project it was found that girls, in particular, who had previously had a very close relationship with their mothers were more likely to be hostile to a new baby – rather than feeling they'd gained a sibling, they felt they'd lost a mother. So when you have a new baby, remember that the bond with your older girl is especially important, and read her cues, so that you can understand what she is feeling. Then you will be able to help address any problems.

Try to get your older child involved with the baby from the start – for example, by letting him or her introduce the new baby to visitors, so that some of the attention is shared. I found it useful to keep a few small gifts on hand, in cases visitors only brought presents for the baby, and I encouraged them to spend some time with my older children before they saw the new member of the family.

Persuading your child to take part in caring for the baby means that he or she will get to know the new-born. But remember that children are individuals, and their attitudes vary: some toddlers love helping to bath or change a baby; others, though, hate the idea – they feel that it's much better to be little and helpless, like the baby, because babies seem to receive more attention. So don't put too much pressure on your child to help you, but just give a little gentle encouragment.

My children felt the idea of having a younger brother or sister more appealing when I provided a few perks to go with their new position – such as a later bedtime, and special visits to the swimming pool to show them that there were all kinds of interesting things that older children could do, but babies couldn't attempt.

Below Your toddler may feel insecure or jealous when with your baby. Make sure that you are always aware of his or her feelings so you can offer comfort.

Left Some toddlers feel important and grown up if they are asked to help look after the baby, and doing so is a good way of showing them that they are still very special to you.

Loosening Ties and Maintaining the Bond

Below Just because you and your child begin to lead independent lives, it doesn't mean that the bond between you will be affected. You will still find that spending time together is very special.

In a large family, it isn't too difficult to loosen the apron strings from the oldest child after a while – after all, the younger children take up a lot of your time and energy and you're probably only too grateful for one child to be relatively independent for at least part of the time. And if both parents work, it's good to see the children – and for them to see you – as separate individuals with particular likes and dislikes; you will be used to your children having lives and friends of their own while you are apart.

But if you are part of a small nuclear family, and have stopped work to care for your children, it may be difficult to recognize that the time has come when your child is no longer a baby who has to be with you all the time. You'll be surprised to discover that he or she has definite views that may not fit in with your own.

Natural characteristics

When your child begins to become more independent, the bond between you is still very important, since it gives your child the confidence to exhibit independence. But just because a secure bond exists, it doesn't mean that your child will automatically be out-going and extrovert – many people, adults as well as children, prefer to listen rather than talk and watch rather than do, and are quiet and self-contained rather than loud and attention-seeking. These characteristics should be respected – they are part of an individual's personality and not the result of poor bonding as a child.

Some children are by nature more timid and shy than others, and such children may be only too happy to stay close to your apron strings. But it's important, that your

child develops the confidence to acquire a degree of independence from you and other people familiar around the house *(see pp.120-123)* before starting school. Make sure your child leaves you occasionally, to learn that it's possible to enjoy things and other people without your presence.

Some children become independent very early on and make up their own minds about who to play with and what to do. You'll soon find you can't take your son or daughter to play with the child of a friend if the two of them don't get on well together. Remember that your child is an independent personality and cannot be treated as an extension of yourself.

Both children and adults develop and change throughout their lives. A child develops very quickly, and his or her needs and interests will change continually as time passes. And adults don't stop developing just because they become parents, but continue to widen their interests as their children become more independent. Sometimes these needs and interests coincide, in which case parents and child can do things together. At other times, however, a compromise will be required. It's important that you neither sacrifice your friends and interests for your children nor constantly insist that your children do things that they dislike.

Left Children should be encouraged to assert their independence, but as every child develops at a different rate you should respect your child's individuality – never feel that there is a competition to be won.

Respecting each other's needs

An older child can understand the likes and needs of others and will respect you more if you are honest about what you want – in any case, it's very nearly impossible to fool a child who knows you well. If you only live for and through your child, this can be quite a burden, especially if it's just at the time that he or she wants to broaden horizons outside the close family unit. Discuss plans with your child and work out ways in which you can both do a bit of what you want, because it's important that a child learns to adapt and compromise. Life is full of compromises, and the earlier a child learns this, the better he or she will fit in well at school and get on with playmates. Show your child that being adaptable is a question of give and take and showing respect for others.

By allowing your child to do what he or she wants some of the time and asking him or her to fit in with your needs at other times, you are not only respecting your child as an individual but also maintaining individuality in your own right. If both of you allow each other the physical and emotional space to be independent at certain times, your mutual bond will be strengthened and you will gradually get to know each other as individuals.

Bereavement, Separation and Divorce

It might be thought that the death of a parent is more devastating in its effect on a small child than a divorce or separation, but this is not the case. In fact, research shows that divorce or separation has a much greater and longer lasting detrimental effect on the psychological health of a child than the death of a father or mother. And researchers have found that whereas anti-social or difficult behaviour in children following bereavement is only marginally more common than average, its incidence at least doubles after divorce or separation. So the two basic phenomena have very different implications, both for the future and for the maintenance and growth of a bond between the surviving or separated parents andtheir children.

Bereavement

When a parent dies, it's inevitable that a young child will grieve, and he or she should be encouraged to do so. But children are often less affected by the death itself than by the emotions displayed and general distress of the surviving parent, both prior to the bereavement (if death was the result of a long illness), and after it. The only answer is to be honest with your child, and talk as naturally and as often as you can about the lost parent and the cause of death – children are much more frightened by silences and secrets than the truth. In fact, children are generally much more resilient than adults, and it seems that the younger the child is, the greater the ability is to adapt to the death of a loved one.

Interestingly, some research demonstrates that children are more affected by the death of the parent of the same sex than by the loss of the opposite-sex parent (though this has not been confirmed by all studies); and in children of both sexes bed-wetting is more common following the death of the mother. So temper your reactions accordingly.

Below Inevitably, death or divorce mean that you will have to make substantial adjustments to your lifestyle, and you should talk about these with your child to help the grieving process and prevent any feelings of guilt.

Separation and divorce

Unfortunately, the break-up of marriages is now so common that it is rare not to know someone who has been through a divorce – as, indeed, I have – though even 30 years ago a divorce would have been thought scandalous. But regardless of the fact that researchers all agree that a child has a significantly better chance of becoming a well-adjusted adult if brought up by both natural parents in a happy, loving atmosphere *(see pp.80-81)*, divorce has become part of today's culture. This book is not about contemporary mores, but the practical aspects of forming and maintaining bonds between children and adults. That being the case, and with divorce being a reality, it's important to think of ways of reducing the detrimental effects of separation on your children.

Regardless of how well your child appears to be handling things, remember that there may be all sorts of problems beneath the surface, because all children find it difficult to

Above Children who are distressed often show signs of insecurity, such as thumb-sucking or clinging.

deal with a divorce. The most important thing you can do to help your child cope is to keep your marital disagreements strictly between you and your partner. Arguing in front of your child will cause more damage than anything else. It's also important that you don't make your child feel that he or she is the cause of your problems. Many children take the guilt the parents feel onto themselves and can very easily become convinced that they are the main reason for the split. "You were happy before I was born" is a difficult statement to refute, so remind your child constantly that the love both you and your ex-partner have for him or her will not diminish in any way.

Reinforce this by trying to put your own worries and problems to one side when you're with your child. Watch him or her carefully for signs of unhappiness and anxiety, such as holding on to a comforter more often, behaving badly, whining, disturbed sleep patterns – or, sometimes, being unnaturally good. When you spot such signs, give your child extra love, affection and attention: hold and touch more often, talk and draw out his or her feelings and thoughts about the split. Do things together, but try to keep to the normal routine and be consistent.

Below Talk to your child about the death of a pet as you would about the death of a human. The suffering he or she feels is similar, and it will be easier to bear if death is not made a taboo.

High emotions

During even the most civilized separations or divorce, emotions run high – and in particular those of guilt and anger: guilt about the failure of the marriage and what you are doing to the children, and anger aimed at both yourself, and, more passionately, your partner. But if you can reinforce and strengthen the mutual bond between you and your child at this time the detrimental effects can be minimalized. That's easy enough to say, of course, but considerable more difficult to do, because your child is likely to be extremely anxious, and will require more affection and attention at a time when you yourself are feeling vulnerable and insecure. The important thing is to avoid dumping all your emotions on your child – remember that it's not his or her fault that you are in this situation and that children soak up the feelings and emotions of those around them like sponges.

So communicate. Listen to what's being said, and watch what's going on. Are your child's true feelings being buried or hidden? Discuss the problems he or she is encountering – if you don't know what they are at this point they will certainly come out later. Maintain a familiar routine to reinforce your child's feeling of security. And – most important of all – keep your efforts up. Research shows that an individual experience, whether good or bad, only rarely has any long-lasting effect on a child. In order to have such an effect, the experience must be continuous and integrated into the child's life: for example, giving short bursts of treatment to children who have behavioural problems or are deprived is ineffective; it is only continuous treatment, over a long period, that works. The analogy is clear: you must pay special attention to your child after a separation, along the lines that I've described, and you must keep up your efforts with consistency for years – in fact, until your child is a child no longer. Goodness knows this is difficult, but it's important that you do your best.

There are several more research findings that you should bear in mind. Studies have shown that boys are more susceptible to long-term psychological damage than girls after a divorce, although why this should be so is not clear. And it also seems that children who are naturally difficult, or who have always behaved badly, are more likely to develop psychological problems – probably because they are more likely to be the target of parental scolding or criticism, which results in poor self-esteem.

Declining standards

One frequent side effect of both bereavement and divorce is an economic and social deterioration in the living standards of the family. If you once took the children swimming every weekend and bought them treat, you probably can't any more. This can cause resentment in a young child, who may not be able to understand the practical realities of the situation. (In my case, I found that my children were able to deal with the divorce itself much more easily than they could handle with the sudden change in lifestyle afterwards.) The confusion the changes create can put a strain on your relationship with your children – sometimes with the result that you feel frustrated and guilty, and find yourself scolding your child for being spoiled, when previously the same requests for treats were accepted.

Above It's vital you maintain a strong bond with your child however upset you're both feeling.

Effects of divorce

During the 1970s and 1980s most experts agreed that children were more affected by the family conflict and tension that often precede and follow a divorce than by the split itself and that if the children were to live in a harmonious home after the parents separated the detrimental effects of the separation would wear off within a few years. In 1993, however, the results were published of a study of a 152 families that appeared to substantially disagree with these findings. Half the families were single-parent ones in which the partners had been separated for at least four years. These children's behavioural problems were contrasted with those of the children that lived with their natural parents in happy, harmonious homes; the children that lived with their natural parents in discordant, argumentative homes; and the children that lived with one parent after a divorce. The results were disturbing – it seems that although a discordant home does result in behavioural problems the incidence is not much over and above the norm, whereas in families where one parent had left home behavioural problems are around five times above the average. Most children of divorced parents of any age, if asked, will state that they would have preferred their parents to have stayed together.

Playing with Peers

Many research projects have looked at how babies interact with the outside world, and an equal number have delved into the reactions of school-age children to authority and friends, but curiously little research has so far been conducted on the behaviour of pre-school children. One or two things are fairly certain, however. We know that children begin to appreciate the emotions and needs of others in their second year (*see pp.120-123*); we also know that young children appear to be cruel to each other at times – from an adult's perspective, that is; and we know how important it is for pre-school children to learn to communicate with their peers and interact with them.

Above School is the great leveller, where children learn that they may not be so highly thought of by playmates as they are by their parents. At this time they have to learn to be adaptable in order to be accepted.

It's natural that a child who feels secure and loved at home will assume that others will treat him or her with the same tolerance and respect, and it may come as a nasty shock if this doesn't happen. Children have little regard for each other's feelings and rarely respect other's emotions, so there are bound to be fights and disagreements when they play. It's much better to allow these to happen without intervening, since children quickly learn how and when to compromise through experience – the learning process isn't nearly as quick if you step into the fray. And most children are keen to learn, because they naturally want to socialize and be accepted, just like most adults.

Family differences

All children have to cope the fact that all families work in different ways, and learn to adapt to the routines of other families. This is one reason why I believe it's important that you're not too rigid about behaviour – if your child has never seen you adapt the rules to differing circumstances, he or she is probably incapable of adjusting to new situations. This ability to adapt becomes very important when a child is learning to play with others. But you can help to make the learning process easier by introducing him or her to other children gradually, from an early age. In fact, this is fairly easy to do: babies like looking at other children and seem to be fascinated by them; and toddlers often play side by side with other small children at first, and later play together with them for short periods. And young children can learn to socialize with their peers through attending toddler groups (*see pp.100-103*) and visiting friends (*see pp.120-123*).

It's very common, too, for a child to create an imaginary friend who can be used to test out social situations and patterns of behaviour, and who fulfils the child's need for companionship. Lydia was such an imaginary friend. She lived with us for a year, and never wanted to go to bed and liked extremely long stories; she was also naughty and used to take biscuits out of the jar. She also used to get upset and had strong views on what she

Left During the toddler years, friendships are made and broken within a matter of days. Provided your child is happy, try not to interfere – it's only if he or she doesn't make friends that you should to ask questions.

wanted to do. I treated Lydia like the other children and ticked her off when she was naughty and explained there was no need to get so upset. Lydia suddenly left us when one of my children started at playschool.

Learning to make friends

In order to make friends, children who are used to playing alone have to try to understand the behaviour of others. They learn through experience and trial and error. Some – usually girls – have a few best friends, while others have a number of less intense friendships. You won't approve of all your children's friends, but don't interfere – remember that the friend you disapprove of may be giving your child something he or she needs. And today's best friend will quite probably be tomorrow's worst enemy.

If your child is having problems making or keeping friendships, stand back and look at the child's personality and relationships within the family. Does your child rule the roost at home? Other children will not allow this. Is your child shy and timid by nature or because he or she feels insecure if separated from you? Reassurance and gentle encouragement is required. Is the child bossy, aggressive and aloof? Other children will sort these problems out for you in time. As children are naturally sociable, a secure child will adapt his or her behaviour to fit in with other children and form friendships quickly.

Above The playground is where the early bonds are tested – whether your child is naturally shy or very outgoing, he or she will not be afraid to join in with others' games, provided there is a secure bond.

Into Proper School

The first day at big school is usually fairly heart-rending for a parent. To a mother or father, the sight of their child going off into the big, wide and often distinctly unfriendly world outside the home seems to mark a watershed: a time when childish innocence is, to an extent, left behind. And a child can look tiny, vulnerable and achingly sweet as he or she gets ready to leave home to take on responsibilities alone and without your guidance and immediate support.

It's understandable that you, as a parent, will feel apprehensive about how your child will take to school: will he or she make friends, fit in, cope with the work and like the teachers? Your child will feel nervous, too – but the nervousness should be tinged with excitement and anticipation at the prospect of new experiences and new friends.

Right The first day at big school is a day of pride and excitement tinged with apprehension – and for the parents, it can be heart-rending.

Practical preparations

Even if what is happening seems like a watershed, there are still practical considerations. Prepare for the first day of school in the same way that you would for the first day at a nursery school or playgroup (*see pp.124-125*). Visit the school together beforehand, meet the teachers and point out what fun school can be. But despite this preparation, it's almost inevitable that you'll be worried about the first day at school, especially if it's your first child – but make sure you don't to let your child sense your anxiety. And if he or she is looking forward to school, encourage this without letting him or her become over-excited. If the school has a uniform, let your child try it on and get used to it a few days before starting school – he or she will probably feel self-conscious but proud of the smart new clothes. Try to do something together as a family as a treat on the evening before, but don't let your child stay awake too late. The first day will be exhausting anyway and your child is more inclined to be upset if he or she is already feeling tired.

Reconcile yourself to the fact that the first day may well be horrible. Arrive at the school early at the end of the day, but close your ears firmly to threats of "I hate it and I'm never going back again". Comfort your child, and let him or her know that you are sympathetic, but that you cannot give in to misery at this stage. Before long, your child should have made new friends and will be progressing into a new stage of life.

Happy reflections

School is a dividing of the ways in both a physical and mental sense. While the child goes somewhere new, the parents stay in their routine, and as a child looks forward to learning about a whole new world, the parents find that they are reflecting on the last few years. I hope that this book will have helped to make this reflection a happy process – that you can think about how you have helped to make your child, happy and secure and ready and eager for new experiences and knowledge, and that the bond you have as a family has helped you and your child feel positive about this new stage in your lives.

Index

D

E

F

G

H

I

J

K

L

Acknowledgements

Morgan Samuel Editions would like to thank the a number of organizations, and all the parents and children who posed as models for this book, and would like to make it clear that none of the photographs of them, or the captions to them, or the context in which they are used in the book, should be taken as any reflection of the actual lifestyle, behaviour or personality of the models themselves.

Thank you to:

Emma Boreham and the staff, children and parents at the Tumbling Tots class at Ealing YMCA, London; Sophie Carter; Sue Carter; Emma Crambton; Kate Crambton; N Crambton; Eve Edmunds; Philippa Edmunds; Catherine Hayes; Zachary Hypolite; Chris Johnston-Brown; Sebastian Johnston-Brown; Cathy Kennedy; Marie Knight at Tomy Babywear; Vivian Lythgoe, Nick Lodge; Thomas Lodge; Megan MacQueen; Charlie Masterson; Jane Masterson; Clare McDowell; James McDowell; Tom McDowell; Heather McPherson; Kelly Mills, Ellie Myers;Sebastian Myers; Tom Perryman; Isabel Pitcaithly-Hill; Jason Pitcaithly-Hill; Aron Singh; Jenny Spurway; Hilary Such at Pools on the Park, Richmond, London, Joanna Sutcliffe; Fiona Talbot-Smith and the staff, parents and pupils at Puffins Nursery School, Fulham, London; Carolyn Valder; Louis Valder; Maggie Wadsworth; Alexander Wilson; Andy Wilson; Amanda Wodhams; Matthew Wolfe; Owen Wolfe; Roshean Wolfe; Amber Wood; Katie Wood; Sam Wood.

Morgan Samuel Editions would also like to thank Jane Wood, for her cups of tea and her styling; Hadas Mills of Kibbutz Representatives for her help; Reg Jeavans, of Wace Corporate Imaging, for his usual good humour; and in particular Andrea Kennedy, the main model in this book, with her son Jamie Oliver Edwards, and Terry Edwards, for her patience and professionalism.

40-588/1